Getting Along With People @ Work

Getting Along With People @ Work
A Guide to Building Better Relationships on the Job

Mary Whelchel

SERVANT PUBLICATIONS
ANN ARBOR, MICHIGAN

Vine Books is an imprint of Servant Publications especially designed to serve
evangelical Christians.

All Scripture quotations, unless indicated, are taken from the HOLY BIBLE,
NEW INTERNATIONAL VERSION® (NIV). Copyright 1973, 1978, 1984 by
International Bible Society. Used by permission of Zondervan Publishing House.
All rights reserved. Scripture quotations identified Phillips are from THE
NEW TESTAMENT IN MODERN ENGLISH, Revised Edition—J.B. Phillips,
translator. © J.B. Phillips, 1958, 1960, 1972. Used by permission of Macmillan
Publishing Co., Inc.

Published by Servant Publications
P.O. Box 8617
Ann Arbor, Michigan 48107

Cover design: Al Furst, Inc., Minneapolis, Minnesota

01 02 03 04 10 9 8 7 6 5 4 3 2 1

Printed in the United States of America
ISBN 1-56955-241-X

Contents

Introduction

The Importance and Challenge of Relationships

Someone has said, "Relationships are the sandpaper of our lives." That sure seems like a fitting description for workplace relationships. Some days we really do feel as though we are being scraped and buffed and ground up by our dealings with abrasive coworkers, impossible managers, and demanding customers!

But as sandpaper is often necessary for a smooth finish, these relationships can indeed be an important part of polishing us, building our character, and developing our potential. For a long time, I've been fond of saying that no one is in our lives by accident. The Bible teaches us that God has sovereign control over everything. Nothing catches him by surprise; everything is filtered to us through his hands. Thus the people we encounter in our jobs—even the ones who have evil intentions or selfish motives or irritating habits—are allowed into our lives by God's providence. There's a reason they are our coworkers or managers or customers.

Scripture tells us, "If it is possible, as far as it depends on you, live at peace with everyone" (Rom 12:18). That's our assignment for all our relationships, including those at work. We are judged by a higher standard than those who have no controlling biblical principles, who have no personal allegiance to Jesus Christ.

Others may live by more commonly accepted relationship principles, such as "Look out for number one!" "Don't take any guff!" and "Stand up for your rights!" They may have no motivation to "live at peace with everyone," but we are called to this Christlike objective. It is a lofty one; it is one that is often out of step with the world's wisdom; it is often not appreciated or valued by others. But for disciples of Jesus Christ, it is the guiding principle.

No doubt you've discovered that you cannot change another person; we can only change ourselves. That means some relationships will never be what we want them to be because the other person is not willing to improve or change. That's when we have to learn to let go and accept the relationship as it is.

However, most relationships can be improved if we work on improving the way we relate. That takes a servant attitude, a willing heart, a dedication to God's principles, and a willingness to be humbled. We have to care more about improving the relationship than proving we are right, getting revenge, or taking care of "number one." But when we choose God's way instead of our own, we discover unimaginable freedom and joy, and the improvement in our relationships is often quite amazing. God's way works—and works the best.

Since we can't change others, only ourselves, in the first chapters we will look at ten important biblical principles that should govern our behavior and attitude toward the people we deal with on our jobs. It's always easy to see how another person needs to change and how wrong he or she is, but our challenge is to take a close look at ourselves and do everything we can to "live at peace with everyone." This means we immediately have to stop blame shifting. We can never ask

God to change others or help us improve our relationships while we are refusing to fulfill what Scripture clearly says is our relationship responsibility.

When you and I intentionally put these principles into practice, it almost always causes a change in the other person. These principles are so becoming and disarming that few can be unaffected by them. So, as you consider each of them, remember that when you choose to practice them, you have everything to gain and nothing to lose. Whether or not the other person responds to your overtures the way you hope, your sense of peace in knowing that you have done what you could to live at peace will be reward enough—especially when you realize you have brought pleasure to the heart of Almighty God. What could be more satisfying?

Chapter 1

Biblical Principle #1

God Created Us With Limits

A great man was speaking to a crowd of thousands, who were hanging on his every word. These people were so eager to hear from him that they were almost trampling each other just to get near him. You see, this was a very great man, held in high esteem by many.

At one point a man in the crowd asked him, "Sir, you are obviously a very wise and great man, and I need a small favor. You see, my brother and I have a long-standing dispute about our inheritance from our father, which he has refused to divide with me as he is supposed to do. Would you please arbitrate this matter? I'm sure he would listen to you, and that would settle the matter quickly."

This great man replied, "Excuse me, but that's not my job! I have not been sent to settle disputes about inheritances. I am not a judge. There are others who are appointed to do those things, but that is not my job." And with that direct, almost abrupt response, he ended that conversation.

I'm sure you recognize that the great man was Jesus Christ. You'll find the story I paraphrased in Luke 12:13-14. Jesus' exact words were: "Man, who appointed me a judge or an arbiter between you?" If you had been Jesus' public relations manager, I think you would have advised Jesus to respond differently. This was not a great PR move for Jesus. He refused to do something he could have done—and could have done quite well—and he refused without explanation, without guilt, and without hesitation.

The Necessity of Boundaries

Had you been the man who made that request, how would you have felt? Perhaps you would have been angry because you were counting on Jesus to resolve this issue. Maybe you would have felt humiliated because you were refused in front of many people. You might have been frustrated because now you had to figure out another way to resolve your problem. Still, Jesus said, "No."

Jesus knew that he had to set reasonable boundaries in his life and ministry here on earth. Without them he would not be able to accomplish what God had sent him to do in just a few short years. By maintaining appropriate boundaries, he stayed focused on his purpose and did not allow others to sidetrack him.

Do you know how to do the same thing for your own life?

A Boundaryless Day

Let me walk you through the day of a hypothetical woman without boundaries in her life, and see how much you can identify with her.

6:00 A.M. The alarm goes off and our woman—we'll call her Betty—stumbles out of bed, dreading the day ahead. *Where is that joy, joy, joy, joy that I'm supposed to have down in my heart?* she thinks to herself. Betty is a believer in Jesus Christ, and with all her heart she wants to be a godly woman. Yet somehow her days are more often filled with frustration than they are with joy.

Then she remembers why she is dreading this day. Yesterday her boss assigned her a new project, one with an unreasonable deadline, and she has to find some way to get it done by five o'clock today.

After a quick shower she goes through the usual morning fight with her teenage son. Getting him out of bed and off to school on time is a constant challenge. He dribbles milk all over the kitchen floor, leaves his room a disaster area, "forgets" to unload the dishwasher (for the third time this week), and breaks the house rules regularly. Betty thinks, "Why can't my son be a little more cooperative? I know he's a teenager, but does that mean he can do exactly what he pleases?"

Betty tries to find a few moments each morning for Bible reading and prayer, but it depends on how things go. If her son is not too much trouble and her husband will help her with a few household chores, she can usually make it. But that's a big "if." Today, of all days, her husband is in a grouchy mood and running late, and he leaves her with all the dishes and picking up a disheveled house.

8:00 A.M. Finally Betty leaves for work, fighting heavy traffic and trying to finish putting on her makeup while she drives. In spite of exceeding the speed limit, she is late for work—

again. "Oh, I'm sure the boss will have something to say about my not being on time—he always does, even though I make it up at lunchtime or by staying late," she says to herself as she runs into the office.

She dives into the project, skipping lunch, working at a fevered pace, and, lo and behold, at 5:00 the project is finished—on time. With great pride she presents her work to her boss, expecting high praise for her accomplishment. But instead he just says, "Good, Betty, I knew you could do it. You always come through for us. Now that you've got that done..." Would you believe it? He has another bright idea, another project, for tomorrow. When will she get her regular work finished?

6:00 P.M. Dejected and exhausted, Betty heads home to face her second job for the day—her family. Rushing through dinner, she tries to get some laundry done that has been piling up for days. She asks for help from her husband and son, but both have other plans. Her husband's plans are to watch a ball game on television, and her son is going to a friend's house! So, with a sigh and suppressed anger, she digs in to get the work done.

Then the phone rings. It's Lori, a friend from church who calls Betty often to complain about her job. Betty knows this means at least a half hour of listening to Lori's woes. Betty wants to be a good friend, but Lori never seems willing to reciprocate. She never listens to Betty's concerns or asks about her situation, yet Lori seems to expect Betty to listen to her own complaints for hours on end. "Oh, well," Betty thinks, "that's what it means to be a good Christian, I guess. Be a servant, Betty."

11:30 P.M. At last Betty falls into bed, exhausted by the end of this rushed, harried day. But she's carrying a lot of things to bed with her: fatigue, anger, self-pity, guilt, and a sense of failure. She works so hard, tries to meet everyone's expectations, and tries to be a good wife, mother, worker, and Christian, but somehow there's no joy in life.

If some of Betty's story sounds too familiar to you, if you see yourself in Betty's shoes too often, then read on! Betty's day was boundaryless, but you can learn the skill of boundary-setting!

What Is a Boundary?
We may not always recognize them, but our lives are full of boundaries. Like fences, signs, walls, hedges, and railings, we need them to keep order in our society, to help prevent harm to individuals and to guard against crime and injustice. Without them we would live in chaos. Some common ones are:

- Stop on red; go on green.
- Work starts at 8:00 A.M. and ends at 5:00 P.M.
- Thou shalt not kill.
- No smoking.
- Curfew: 10:00 P.M.
- Danger! Do not enter!

You may notice that the examples I just gave have been set by law or other authorities in our lives, or they reflect accepted practice in our society. What many of us have never recognized is that we must also set personal boundaries if we are to avoid chaos and harm in our lives. This does not mean that we build walls between others and ourselves or live in isolation, nor does it mean that we live self-centered lives. It simply means that we recognize and understand where we must draw the lines that say, "Here and no more," not because we are selfish or lazy but because we will never accomplish what God has called us to do without these boundaries.

Workplace Boundaries

A good friend who works in a Christian organization recently asked me if she had a right to set boundaries in her relationship with her boss. An executive in the organization had told her that she did not have this right, especially since her boss was a Christian. She should just do whatever he asked and assume that was what God wanted her to do.

As I told my friend, I completely disagree. Even Christian bosses don't always know where appropriate boundaries are in dealing with employees. Setting necessary boundaries is your right—and responsibility—though it must be done with great care and preparation.

Identifying Your Own Workplace Boundary Needs

Boundary challenges may occur in any on-the-job relationship: the person who constantly stops by your desk just to chat; the constant gossip or complainer about the company; the individual who interrupts you frequently to ask questions he or she could have answered alone; the colleague who is habitually late, or who spends far too much time on personal telephone calls; the boss who expects you to work late without prior notice or good reason.

I could go on and on, but it will be more helpful to you to

think about your own workplace and make up your own list. Write down the challenges you identify, and while you're at it, think about the degree of control you actually have in the particular situation—fairly complete control, limited control, or none. For instance, if you include the fact that your boss works in crisis mode and gives you work at the last minute, you might mark that as a situation where you have limited control.

Once you have done this little exercise, you are ready to start thinking about how you can actually start setting some helpful boundaries.

Boundary-Setting Methods

Verbal Boundaries

Boundaries are most often set with words. The most basic one is "no." It is not a bad word; it is a necessary word. Jesus said, "Simply let your 'Yes' be 'Yes' and your 'No,' 'No'; anything beyond this comes from the evil one" (Mt 5:37). In other words, "no" should be a word in your vocabulary that you use at appropriate times, with clarity, so no one can misunderstand you.

It's not a bad idea to practice your "no" responses. Think of how you could say no in the least negative way in the situations you just identified.

- "I'm sorry, but I can't help you right now. Can I come to your office in ten minutes, when I've finished this?"
- "No, I won't be able to work late tonight. However, if I have your data by 3:00, the report should be ready for your meeting tomorrow."

- "I can't talk right now. Why don't we have coffee later this week and catch up?"

If you get some words and phrases in your mind ahead of time, you're more likely to handle it well when the time comes that they are needed.

It's also good to remember that you can say "no" simply by making positive statements. For example:

- "You can find that answer by looking in the software manual."
- "Sure, I'll be glad to help as soon as I have this report finished."
- "We can meet that deadline as long as the quarterly reports can be postponed by a week."

Nonverbal Boundaries

Always remember that your body language speaks louder than your words. I learned something about this when I was a young sales representative for IBM, one of the first women in that position. When I began, my manager warned me to expect some male customers to make passes, yet after a few months I realized (thankfully) that this was not happening. It almost made me wonder if something was wrong with me!

I finally mentioned this to the manager one day when we were out making calls together. He replied, "Mary, it is obvious when you walk into a customer's office that you are there to get an order, and the way you handle yourself sends the message that you don't have time for messing around."

I realized I *was* very focused on doing my job and getting my quota each month. Without even realizing it, my professional demeanor and "let's get down to business" body language had set a boundary that was clearly recognized by my customers.

You can make this phenomenon work for you in many situations. The following are just a couple of the boundary challenges you may encounter, with ways you might meet them.

You have a critical deadline, and you need three hours of uninterrupted time in order to meet it. One simple strategy is to turn off your e-mail and possibly your phone. You wouldn't want to do this except when most necessary, but it could make all the difference. Similarly, you might simply shut your office door, if you have one.

Your office or cubicle is in a busy traffic pattern, and people often stop to chat. Again, one possibility is simply to close your office door, if you have one. If, like many of us, this is not possible, try remembering a handy little fact of communication. When you make eye contact, you are giving the other person permission to engage in conversation. When you realize your "chatty Kathy" is approaching you, try keeping your eyes focused on your computer screen or the papers on your desk, *looking* deeply involved in your work, and don't look up if you can avoid it.

Sometimes, if it is possible, rearranging furniture is a big help, especially if your talkative colleague sits nearby. Make it so you're not facing people casually walking by—or sitting nearby, too ready to talk. You may even find that your department head or office manager is happy to see such rearrangements made discreetly in the name of efficiency or productivity—they may solve a problem for him or her too!

Mental Boundaries

So much of our success in boundary-setting, as well as every-thing else, begins and ends in our thought life. Paul recommends our "taking captive every thought to make it obedient to Christ" (2 Corinthians 10:5).

This is a topic of great importance, and more than can be covered in depth here. My book *What Would Jesus Think?* gives much help in learning how to do this.

You may work with a person who tries to upset you with accusations, condemnation, or guilt trips. Yet his or her strategy will work only if you allow yourself to dwell on the invading words. When you think about harsh, unkind, rude words, you are likely to become disturbed, upset, or angry. By controlling your thoughts, you set a boundary that limits what you allow into your mind.

Pushing out wrong thoughts by replacing them with right thoughts is not a skill that can be mastered overnight, but it can be learned and can have considerable effect on your emotional health.

Recently a young woman was telling me about a close relative who knows how to use words like bullets, often being quite hurtful, and loves to lay guilt trips on my friend. I reminded my friend that her relative's words can hurt her only when she is thinking about them. Therefore, her challenge is to replace that wrong thinking with right thinking. My friend has a wonderful husband and many blessings in her life. I encouraged her to start counting her blessings—out loud if possible—every time those hurtful words start to replay in her mind.

The pain she is experiencing is deeply rooted, as she has had to endure it for many years. It will take some time for her to master a new way of handling those verbal attacks, but like all of us, she has the ability to set a mental boundary that will keep those words and comments out of her mind. If she is not thinking about them, they can't hurt her.

Another woman told me a sad story about how a customer had verbally abused her. The event had occurred eighteen months earlier, yet her voice began to shake as she told me the story. It was obvious she was still experiencing the trauma of that earlier time.

Realizing that she had never learned how to set mental boundaries, I told her, "You have to let this go. Rude customers go with the territory, and you're taking this very personally." She protested, "But he was so awful!" "I'm sure he was," I replied, "but you're allowing him to hurt and rehurt you every day because you remember it and think about it daily."

If you don't know how to set mental boundaries, you will inflict ongoing pain and misery on yourself. You can't control what other people say or do, but you can control how much of your thought life it occupies.

Boundaries for the Boss

There are times when you may need to set a boundary in your relationship with your boss. This presents an interesting challenge, but it can be done if you approach it the right way. Here are some tips.

Pray for the right attitude before you make a move. Don't express yourself in a way that is demanding or rude. Show your boss respect, and you are more likely to be treated with respect.

Offer alternatives and assure management of your willingness and desire to do your job right. In our hypothetical example, Betty might have pointed out her difficulties in getting her work done and said, "If I do this special project for you in the time frame you ask, I will not be able to complete my normal work. Could you give me a little more time to do this? Alternatively, would it be OK with you if I miss some other commitments as a result?"

Set limits. Let your boss know how much you can do and how quickly you can do it. If accomplishing the new task means putting aside previously assigned work, let him or her know this, and ask your boss to set the priorities.

Ask for clarification of duties and priorities. Often bosses are not good at giving clear instructions or communicating their priorities. That can be very frustrating as well as unproductive. Let your boss know that you want to do the best job possible and meet his or her expectations. Suggest a set time each day or each week simply to go over schedule, workload, or priorities with him or her in order to avoid wasted time. You might cite a recent occasion when not knowing the boss's priorities caused you to miss a deadline.

Where Should We Set Boundaries?

This is a difficult question to answer because no two situations and no two people are alike. So we will need to ask God for wisdom.

The Christian life is a process. We are in the process of being transformed into the likeness of Jesus Christ with ever-increasing glory, as we read in 2 Corinthians 3:18. That means we will grow in our ability to set appropriate boundaries.

Such growth does not happen overnight, however. If we have lived without boundaries for a long time, changing our habits and hearing God's voice on a daily basis may take us some time. But the sooner we begin the process of change, the sooner we will get out of the boundaryless lifestyle that leads to so much burnout, stress, and anger, and worst of all, missing the good things God has planned for us to do.

Ephesians 2:10 tells us, "For we are God's workmanship, created in Christ Jesus to do good works, which God prepared in advance for us to do." God has a plan for your life. He certainly intends for you to be busy, and at times you will get weary and tired, but if you live within wise boundaries, you will be able to stay focused on doing what he wants you to do and not be trying to jump through everyone else's hoops.

How do you know what good works God has for you to do? That comes through getting to know God more and more through his Word and through prayer and meditation. I recommend that you begin each day praying Romans 12:1 and 2 into your life, like this:

Lord, today I present my body to you as a living sacrifice. May it be holy and pleasing to you today. I offer this as my spiritual act of worship. Help me not to be conformed today to the pattern of this world, but transform me by renewing my mind. In that way, Lord, today I can test and approve what is your will for me today—your good, pleasing, and perfect will.

Then, as you spend time each day in the Bible, look for principles about boundaries. The Spirit of God will point them out to you. The following are just two examples of what you will find.

The rest principle. God set up specific boundaries for the children of Israel concerning when they were to work and when they were to rest. He made it clear that one day out of seven was needed for bodily and mental rest. That is a boundary that was put in place for good reasons. It is the way God made us. Do you rest one in seven days?

The heart principle. Wise Solomon gave us a high-priority principle here: "Above all else, guard your heart, for it is the wellspring of life" (Prv 4:23). The word "heart" is used here as it often is in Scripture, to identify the seat of our thoughts and our emotions. We are to guard that center—put some boundaries around it. What does that mean? The answer may vary according to our stage of life or particular circumstances at the time.

For a single person, it may mean being very careful how you allow your heart to become attached or involved with potential mates. If you make a poor choice in this area, you will bring much pain and suffering on yourself.

For others it will mean being careful what you allow into your mind because you will become what you think and you will think about what you feed into your mind. If someone is trying to invade your heart through guilt, accusations, criticism, or belittling, you may have to set some emotional or physical boundaries to keep that person from inflicting unnecessary pain on you.

Meditate on this verse, and ask God to show you where you need to "guard your heart." He may have some very specific things in mind that are important for your particular life.

Not long ago a very successful young female executive called me in distress over some unfair and unprofessional treatment she was currently encountering. After talking with her, I recognized that her "heart" was very much entwined with her position and success in the business world. She was understandably ambitious and desirous of moving higher in her large company, and this perceived threat was causing her great concern and turmoil.

She is a dedicated follower of Jesus Christ, so I gently reminded her that she needed to "guard her heart" to make sure that the job never became her highest priority—never took first place in her heart. If being successful by corporate standards is more important to her than being successful by God's standards, she will find her heart frequently disturbed. By "guarding her heart" and making certain that her priorities are biblically in line, she can trust that even these unpleasant and unfair circumstances have some purpose that God can turn into good for her.

Two Kinds of Boundaries

We need to set two types of boundaries in our lives, ones that govern our own living and others that affect the behavior of persons with whom we work or have other relationships.

Personal Boundaries
This is one area where we do have control, and I've discovered that when my own personal boundaries are in good shape, it is much easier to address the boundaries needed in my relationships with others.

Mental boundaries. These determine what we will and will not allow ourselves to think about and thus what attitude we will take into our day. This in turn influences what we say.

Physical boundaries. For our best possible state of well-being, we set guidelines for ourselves regarding how much sleep we will get and how much exercise we put into our schedule, as well as dietary boundaries.

Emotional boundaries. We also have considerable control over what we will and will not get angry about—and how long we will stay angry. In other words, we can determine what we will and will not spend our emotional energy on. (My rule of thumb: If it doesn't matter in twenty-four hours, I am not allowed to spend any emotional energy.)

As I read the Bible, I find many guidelines for personal boundaries that need to be in my life. For instance:

Be quick to listen and slow to speak.

JAMES 1:19b

Do not let any unwholesome talk come out of your mouths, but only what is helpful for building others up according to their needs, that it may benefit those who listen.

EPHESIANS 4:29

Be thankful.

COLOSSIANS 3:15b

Do everything without complaining or arguing.

PHILIPPIANS 2:14

Boundaries in Our Relationships With Others

Again, the Bible has very relevant guidelines for us as we determine where we need to set boundaries in our relationships with people at work. The following are just a few of them.

Don't waste your breath on fools, for they will despise the wisest advice.

PROVERBS 23:9, NLT

When arguing with fools, don't answer their foolish arguments, or you will become as foolish as they are.

PROVERBS 26:4, NLT

Those who oppose [the Lord's servant] he must gently instruct, in the hope that God will grant them repentance leading them to a knowledge of the truth.

2 TIMOTHY 2:25

Communicating Our Relationship Boundaries

Some of the boundaries we set serve principally as directions to ourselves, ways in which we manage our own inner lives. For example, we may determine not to let a particular person lay guilt trips on us. Or we may decide to intentionally disregard another's judgments because we have found his thinking is often inaccurate or ineffective. This kind of boundary does not have to be communicated verbally to the other person involved.

On the other hand, there *are* boundaries that directly involve our work with others or our expectations of them. (See the following section about the mistakes Betty made.) To prevent misunderstanding or ongoing frustration, these need to be communicated in ways appropriate to the situation. For instance, we may need to let our boss know that we have decided to limit our overtime hours because of the negative impact on our family life. Or we may need to ask our employees to schedule time for needed discussions in order to avoid multiple interruptions each day. And though we do hope it will not be necessary, occasionally we must set ethical boundaries, such as refusing to knowingly falsify any work or lie, even for our boss.

Boundary Mistakes

As you read about Betty's boundaryless day, you no doubt perceived some critical mistakes she made that led to the mess she was in. It would be easy to blame her problem on her son or her husband or her boss or her friend, but in actuality Betty has allowed others to take advantage of her. She wanted her son to be more responsible. She even outlined some household duties for him, but those were not enforced, and he was allowed to continue taking advantage of her at will. Betty and her husband had not communicated about the division of responsibilities in their home, and she allowed him to place the whole load on her shoulders. And because she never said "no" to her demanding boss and somehow managed to meet his unrealistic expectations, he simply raised the bar and expected more. Furthermore, just as many people do in a misguided attempt to be "nice" and out of false guilt, Betty gave her friend tacit permission to treat her like a doormat.

You can't blame Betty for not trying. You can't say she didn't have a good heart or even good motivations. But you certainly can say that Betty had never learned to set boundaries. She had mistaken ideas of what her responsibilities were in various relationships and as a result allowed others to impose unfair and unrealistic demands on her. In fact, she enabled these relationships to continue to be unbalanced, to her own detriment. And because these people in her life were allowed to get by with wrong behavior, they never learned where they needed to grow and change themselves.

In spite of the fact that she has been trying to make everybody happy and keep all of her relationships in good shape, Betty is headed for disaster. If she does not set some boundaries soon, resentment and anger will build up until they emerge in totally uncontrollable ways and at inappropriate times. Her health will suffer. Her walk with God will be harmed. Even the relationships she has been trying to foster will be harmed.

Unfortunately, many of us make the same kinds of mistakes as Betty has.

Mistake: Failure to Clearly Identify Your Boundaries

Have you ever tried to communicate your boundaries in a rational, nonemotional, nonangry manner? A good way to begin is to write those boundaries out until they are phrased appropriately. Be sure they are based on biblical principles, not on your own selfish needs or desires.

Whether or not you share these with others depends on the relationship and situation, but just the act of writing them out will solidify them in your own mind and give you a helpful reference and reminder.

Some of the boundaries our friend Betty desperately needs to put in writing might look like the following.

Boundary #1. I will not be responsible for getting my son to school on time. I will remind him once and once only that it is time to get up. If he is late, he will have to deal with the consequences.

Boundary #2. I will not work through my lunch hour more than one day each week. I will take my lunch break and use it as a time to refocus my mind and give myself a needed breather.

Boundary #3. I will not take on added work assignments without informing my boss of the impact it will have on my time and insisting that he choose between the various assignments when he gives me more than can be done in the time allotted.

Boundary #4. I will make a list of daily household chores and ask my husband and son to designate which ones they will assume. That list will be posted on the refrigerator, and I will *not* do their jobs when they fail to do them. Neither will I nag them about doing their jobs. Those jobs will simply be left undone.

Mistake: Failure to Communicate Boundaries

Many people have set boundaries in their own minds for their relationships with others but have never found the right way to communicate those boundaries. The people exceeding your boundaries may be totally oblivious to what they are doing because you have never communicated what the boundaries are.

Carefully and with love, you need to let them know where you stand. That will take wisdom, and it may mean a confrontation. It may even produce some unpleasant temporary results, but the longer you put it off, the worse it gets.

If you will take the time to put your boundaries in writing, you may find it a very helpful tool as you try to communicate them. Talking about them with others can be uncomfortable, especially if you are confrontation-adverse—like me! Having something in writing with you will serve several purposes: it will show that you have given this lots of thought; it will indicate your seriousness; and it will help keep you on track when you are talking so that your nerves don't cause you to forget or say something wrong.

It is extremely important that you don't try to communicate boundaries on the spur of the moment or when you are angry. That almost always causes bigger problems. Chapter seven (on confrontation) will be helpful at this point, as you must choose the right words, the right time, and the proper attitude to do this.

Mistake: Movable Boundaries

People with movable boundaries—boundaries that change depending on the situation—are easy to spot. There are two common types.

The overly compliant. There are those who give in to others easily, who always say yes, who never "rock the boat." Whatever someone else asks becomes the boundary at that moment. They try very hard to please; they want to be accepted; they want everyone to be happy with them. So they move their boundaries when necessary to accommodate anyone and everyone.

"Compliants" take on too many responsibilities and do not set clear boundaries because they live in fear of hurting others' feelings, fear of someone else's anger, fear of punishment, fear of being unspiritual. Fear is a daily component of their lives.

While Christians certainly should be loving, giving people, biblical compliance is easily distinguished from harmful compliance. Biblical compliance comes from a heart of compassion, not a sense of fear. It does not produce anger or resentment.

The apathetic or unconvinced. People who lack strong convictions and commitments tend to have movable boundaries. For example, a single person may determine not to become involved with anyone who is not a fellow believer, but those boundaries change when an attractive person shows interest. Movable boundaries are a recipe for disaster.

Boundaries Are Spiritual

Setting boundaries is not a selfish act. Jesus set boundaries in his life: limiting his exposure to people, limiting his time with people, and limiting the things he was willing to do. And he did so not because he was selfish but because he was determined to do what the Father had sent him to do. As a result, at the end of a short, three-year ministry, he could say, "I have brought you glory on earth by completing the work you gave me to do" (Jn 17:4).

Setting reasonable, biblical boundaries is a most spiritual thing to do if we do it for the right reason, and that reason is so that we can accomplish what God wants us to do and be able to say as Jesus did, "I have brought glory to God on earth by completing the work he gave me to do."

I urge you to make boundary-setting an intentional part of your life. Pray about it. Ask God to reveal the areas in your life that need boundaries. Read the Bible and look for biblical principles concerning your boundaries. Believe me, they are there, and God will reveal them to you if you will seek for them with all your heart.

But remember, the reason for setting boundaries must be primarily to bring glory to God while we are here on earth.

A Boundary Checkup

Here's a quick checklist to help you evaluate your Boundary IQ. Is each statement true or false for you?

True | False
☐ | ☐

I too often take responsibility for family members, friends, or coworkers instead of requiring them to take responsibility for themselves.

True | False
☐ | ☐

I feel guilty when I refuse a request, so I rarely say no.

True | False
☐ | ☐

I have great difficulty confronting people, so I often end up doing what they want in order to avoid a scene.

True | False
☐ | ☐

I communicate my boundaries when I am angry and then back down later because of losing my temper.

True | False
☐ | ☐

I am reluctant to ask for help from other people.

True | False
☐ | ☐

If someone is unhappy with me, I immediately figure it is my fault and try my best to make them happy.

True | False
☐ | ☐

I seem to find much of my identity in the praise of others, so I am far too willing to do anything in order to win their approval.

True | False
☐ | ☐

I go out of my way to do things for other people in order to win their friendship or approval.

True   False

☐   ☐   I expect the people closest to me to know my boundaries even though I never have clearly communicated them.

True   False

☐   ☐   I feel as though many people take advantage of me, pushing me beyond my boundaries, and I harbor resentment and anger toward them for it.

If you were candid in this checkup, it may give you some insight into your Boundary IQ—how much work you have yet to do! Grade yourself:

Number of "True" Answers	Your Boundary IQ
1	Excellent
2 to 4	Good
5	So-So
6 to 9	Poor
10	Dreadful

Even if your Boundary IQ is in bad condition, take heart! You too can learn to set boundaries, and as Christians we have a great advantage because we have the power of God's Spirit living in our body, we have the mind of Christ, and we have the ever-abiding love of God our Father. These provide motivation and power for us to do what otherwise might be difficult or impossible.

Personal Performance Review

I strongly recommend that you begin putting some boundaries in writing and then start praying about those boundaries.

Part I. Personal Boundaries

Can you think of any areas in your life in which you need to set (or strengthen) healthy personal boundaries? Make three lists, one under each of the following headings:

> *Physical (Health-Related) Boundaries*
> *Emotional (Relational) Boundaries*
> *Mental (Attitude-Related) Boundaries*

Part II. Boundaries for Others

Are you enabling others, in your family or at work, to avoid the consequences of their own inappropriate behavior because you do too much for them? Are you experiencing false guilt because you are trying to jump through hoops that were never meant for you? Are you trying to win approval by proving that you are a "superwoman" or "superman"? Are you afraid to confront those in your life who continually invade your territory and push the envelope? On a piece of paper, write about them under the following headings: *Family Issues, Work Issues.*

Chapter 2

Biblical Principle #2

Put Others First

There was a very wealthy man who was moving his family and all his earthly possessions to another country, as God had directed him to do. His nephew and his family were going with him. This nephew was very much inclined to "take care of number one," to make sure he got the best deal possible.

At one point it became obvious that the two of them needed to part ways and travel separately. Quarreling had arisen between these two families over what belonged to whom, and there was so much strife between them that it definitely seemed best for this rich man to go one way and his nephew to go another.

In a wonderful example of putting others first, the rich man allowed his nephew to choose which way he wanted to go; he would take what was left over. The nephew, ever careful to get the best deal possible, chose the best way, the richest way, the easiest way.

At that point it must have seemed that the nephew was the winner and the rich, generous uncle had been cheated. But we know the end of that story: the rich uncle received a promise from God that he would have great success and his offspring would form a new nation, a people made for God.

This man was, of course, Abram, and you'll find the story in Genesis 13:1-18. And that wasn't the last time Abram voluntarily put Lot first, ahead of his own interests. He bailed him out of captivity in Sodom and Gomorrah (Gn 14) and pleaded for his deliverance from God's judgment on Sodom and Gomorrah (Gn 18:22-33).

Abram (later called Abraham) was willing to put others first, and God blessed him richly. The rewards weren't immediately evident. In fact, they were delayed for quite some time. But in God's perfect timing, Abraham knew God's rich blessing on himself and his family.

The Meaning of "Put Others First"

This passage gives a very good definition of what it means to put others first:

> Do nothing out of selfish ambition or vain conceit, but in humility consider others better than yourselves. Each of you should look not only to your own interests, but also to the interests of others.
>
> PHILIPPIANS 2:3-4

The King James Version of this passage says "esteem" others better than yourself. The Phillips translation says, "In humility think more of one another than you do of yourselves." So it's clear that putting others first has to do with our attitude toward other people, with the way we see them, with the respect we give them.

From birth onward we are for the most part quite focused

on—and proficient at—putting ourselves first, so this will require more power and motivation than we normally have within ourselves. It definitely will need to be a God-thing.

Paul continues by describing what it looks like to "put others first." He says, "Your attitude should be the same as that of Christ Jesus" (Phil 2:5), and he defines this Christlike attitude in verses 6 through 8: that of a servant, humble, unselfish, obedient to God.

The best way to describe what putting others first looks like is to tell you about my friend Cindy (not her real name). She is a schoolteacher in a challenging environment. The principal is notoriously difficult. No one gets along with her, and she receives neither the respect nor the loyalty that one in her position should.

On Cindy's first day, her coworkers told her that getting along with the principal was "mission impossible." She soon understood what they meant, as she found the principal to be arrogant, aloof, demanding, unrealistic, incompetent—you get the point. After a spiritual struggle of her own, Cindy decided it was her job to get along with this woman and by God's grace she would certainly try.

Cindy had many opportunities to learn to live by the put-others-first principle. She had to learn to keep her mouth shut when she wanted to be defensive, do everything possible to meet the principal's demands, do her best to carry out her responsibilities whether it was ever appreciated or not. In other words—putting the principal's interests ahead of her own.

Soon it became obvious that Cindy was able to get along with this authority figure while no one else could. She's been asked what she had to do to get this principal to be kind to her. Others incur the principal's wrath and criticism, but Cindy no longer receives this treatment. Cindy sees this as a bonus, as she was not expecting the relationship to improve; she was just determined to obey the Lord. Now she tells of how easy it is for her to work for this person—even enjoyable—though the other teachers and staff still have trouble.

Cindy's secret is simply that she adopted the same attitude that Paul described as that of Jesus. She humbled herself and accepted even demeaning treatment from the principal. She forgot about trying to get her own way or prove she was right, instead doing her best to get along with her boss. She took a servant attitude, going the extra mile and being willing to do some of the "dirty work" and to be unappreciated. And most of all, she acted out of obedience to the Lord, desiring to please him, rather than some other principle of "correctness"—and this made it all possible.

"Putting others first" will look different in different situations and relationships, but Jesus' attitude is always the gold standard. If you can compare your own attitude to his and see a likeness, then you are on the right track.

"Put Others First" Does Not Mean "Put Yourself Down"

It's important to avoid this misunderstanding. In fact, when we truly put others first, we discover an unexpected harvest of joy and personal fulfillment. The happiest people I know are those who are continually putting others first. It's one of those biblical paradoxes, where we win by losing.

The reason for this result is that we are not so focused on ourselves. As I often remind myself, *self* is not my solution, it is my problem. In a time when words beginning with "self-" are filling up our dictionaries, this is something we must continually relearn. Focusing too much on ourselves is only a recipe for unhappiness.

In Philippians 2 Paul says we should look *not only* to our own interests. There is an implied understanding that looking to our own interests is not forbidden but is to be kept in proper balance with our concern for others.

How to Put Others First

Now the question becomes, how in the world do we put this into practice in our everyday lives? I remember when I first started to take this passage seriously. It bothered me greatly because I couldn't see how in the world I could ever *feel* that other people were better or more important than I am. I might talk that way or try to act that way, but how could I ever feel that way *in my heart?*

That's where I made my mistake. Paul didn't say I should *feel* that other people are better or more important than I am. Feelings will often lead us astray, and they are unreliable gauges of our hearts and our wills. Just because we don't feel a certain way or have an emotional motivation doesn't necessarily mean our heart attitude is wrong.

Paul said we are to *consider* others better than ourselves, *esteem* them to be so. That is a mind attitude, not an emotional feeling. That is a choice you and I can make at any time in any relationship.

In order to put others first, what I needed was a changed

way of thinking about others and myself. But how to make that happen? That was my next challenge. And if I didn't feel it, how could I know that I truly had a changed attitude?

Prayer First

I began to realize that this attitude change could only come through prayer and through the power of God's Spirit within me. I recognized it would never be possible for me, in my own selfish nature, to make this happen. This had to be a God-thing if it were ever to be a reality.

So I began to pray it into my life. Daily I would pray something like this: "Lord, whomever I deal with today, help me to think of them as more important than me; help me to put their interests ahead of my own." Let me tell you what started to happen. People began to look different to me. I would remember throughout my day, *Mary, they have problems and concerns that are just as important to them as yours are to you.* And when I'd find myself irritated with someone, the Holy Spirit would remind me of my prayer and I would recognize that I needed this attitude change.

New Thought Patterns

My normal thought patterns run this way: *This person has no right to upset me, or interfere with my schedule, or invade my space, or ask this of me. Doesn't he [or she] understand that what I am doing is very important?*

Whereas before I had indulged in these thought patterns without recognizing how wrong they were, now that convicting voice of God's Spirit wouldn't let me get by with that kind of thinking any longer. I'd remember, "Think of their interests as more important than your own."

At that point I had a choice: to obey or not to obey. When I chose to obey and allowed God's Spirit to change my attitude, then I could see that person from a totally different perspective. I could honestly set my will to treat that person as though his or her situation and interests were important and mine could be put on the back burner temporarily while I dealt with that person.

When I did not obey, I behaved and reacted as before—with frustration, irritation, stress, and selfishness. That kind of reaction never improved a relationship but rather did just the opposite. Even if I tried to cover up my true feelings, it would be obvious through my body language and tone of voice that I did not think that person's situation was as important as mine.

Does it work every time? Yes, it does—every time I remember to pray it into my life and am willing to relinquish my rights to the Holy Spirit. Do I practice it all the time without fail? Unfortunately not, but I'm learning. As long as I pray it in, it will become more and more of a reality. When I don't do that, I lose the focus.

Right Motivation

I am motivated to do this by my love for Jesus and desire to please him, not by others making me want to do it. If we wait for other people to motivate us or appreciate what we do, this will always be mission impossible.

This is one of the major lessons we have to keep relearning as we seriously strive to obey God's Word. It is a matter of our will, not our feelings. Don't worry if you don't *feel* like thinking more highly of others than yourself. Instead set your will to *think* of others as more important and to act and react from that mindset. You will discover that, in spite of your feelings, your behavior will change and eventually it will start to change your feelings.

Philip Yancey, in his book *Reaching for the Invisible God,* advises that it is easier to act your way into feelings than to feel your way into actions. In other words, do what you know is right to do and let the feelings follow, if they will. If you wait on your feelings to kick in before you do what you know you should do, you'll be in wait mode many days, if you're like me!

This is such an important principle of the Christian life that it cannot be overstated. We live by faith, not by sight. We do what we know is right to do by faith, often in direct opposition to our human sight or desires. We obey out of love for God and a desire to please him, not because our feelings or emotions motivate us to do so. When I remember to act my way into feelings instead of waiting on my feelings to act, God is able to impart the grace that I need to do what looks like an impossibility.

Personal Performance Review

Here is a checkup list to help you see how you're doing in the "put others first" department. Which of these statements do you find true for you?

- I get upset easily when someone interrupts my schedule or interferes with my plans.
- I am very protective of my space and time and resent people who invade them unnecessarily.
- When other people are talking to me about themselves, I can easily tune them out.
- I become irritated with people who tell me details about their lives that I don't need or want to know.
- I consider my time very valuable and work hard not to let anyone waste my time.
- In most of my conversations, I do more talking than listening.
- I'm very focused on getting the job done and have little patience with people who are not project-oriented.
- I feel that many people spend their lives in shallow pursuits, and what they have to say is usually trivial.
- I usually have a very good reason for not giving people the time or attention they seem to want.
- It seems to me that too many people just don't have anything important to do, and I can't afford to let them waste my time because I have lots of important things to do!

If those ten statements fit you too closely, you're not the Lone Ranger! They are all too much just like me! That's how I could write them; I know what I'm like. However, by God's grace you can change and become more focused on others and more caring about their lives, if you truly want to.

By the way, it doesn't require a personality change. Even if you're not a "people person," you can learn to put others first.

But you will have to become intentional about it. So, if you're ready to obey Jesus by putting another's welfare ahead of your own, execute the following plan and watch your own transformation!

A Plan for Putting Others First

Who is the most difficult person you encounter on your job? Write down the name on a piece of paper.

Next, decide what you could do to have—and demonstrate—the same attitude Jesus had, to put this other person first. The following questions may help you.

- Are you willing to pray a Christ-attitude into your heart out of obedience to the Lord God?
- What could you do for this person that would exceed his or her expectations?
- What could you do for this person that would puncture your pride and cause you to humble yourself?
- What could you do for this person that you may not want to do but that would benefit the person?
- Is there some "lowly" thing you could do for him or her that you might even consider beneath you?

Once you have come up with a few things you can do that would be putting the other person first, select one or two and make them part of your daily "to do" list. In fact, actually write them on your calendar or enter them into your Palm Pilot, to remind you to carry out your intentions.

Chapter 3

Biblical Principle #3

Rejoice and Weep With Others

There was a woman who had longed to have a baby, but she had never been able to conceive, though she and her husband had prayed much for a child. Then, in the later years of her biological clock, she found that she was pregnant, and she was overjoyed.

In the sixth month of her pregnancy, a young relative came to visit and announced that she too was pregnant. In fact, she was going to give birth to the Messiah.

On hearing this news, the older woman actually shouted with joy and blessed her young relative, celebrating the best of all news, that she had been chosen to bear God's Son. You see, this woman knew how to rejoice over another's good news without envy or resentment.

I'm talking about Elizabeth and Mary, of course. You'll find this visit recorded in Luke 1.

You know, it would have been understandable if Elizabeth had felt a tinge of jealousy. After all, she was older, more mature, and a godly woman with a godly husband. Why didn't God choose her for this most blessed assignment? But you find none of that in Elizabeth. She knew how to rejoice with Mary and thereby increase her own joy.

It is my opinion that Mary went to see Elizabeth even before she announced her unusual pregnancy to her family. I think she knew that Elizabeth would rejoice with her and not be suspicious or envious. It took a few days to travel from Nazareth to Elizabeth's home near Jerusalem. It was not an easy journey back then, but Mary needed someone to rejoice with her, and she knew Elizabeth would be that kind of friend.

The apostle Paul very succinctly summed up the principle at work here: "Rejoice with those who rejoice; mourn with those who mourn" (Rom 12:15). We've heard the phrase "I feel your pain" so often in the last few years that for many people it has become a sarcastic cliché. Certainly, if it is associated with phoniness or insincerity, or it is perceived as a manipulative ploy, it loses its meaning.

However, this biblical principle is not only about feeling others' pain but sharing in their joys and happiness. In any relationship where we truly rejoice and mourn with each other, the bond between us is strengthened enormously. A oneness of spirit is created, and we lighten each other's burdens as well as enhance each other's happiness.

Rejoicing With Others

Have you ever been excited and told a friend some good news, only to discover that he or she didn't seem to find it exciting at all? I remember once long ago when my company had advised me that I was to go to a special conference. This was an honor in our company, and I was thrilled.

I immediately shared it with my friend and coworker,

expecting her to be happy with me. Instead my good news put her into a terribly bad mood; she didn't speak to me for quite a while. You see, she also wanted to go to the conference, so instead of rejoicing with me, she was angry and jealous. Her reaction took a lot of the joy away from me by making me feel guilty for even having good news.

I imagine something like that has happened to you, and you know how it feels. Not very good! I really believe most of us find it easier to mourn with someone than to rejoice because that old green-eyed monster, jealousy, raises his ugly head and we wish that something good would happen to us.

Have you ever had thoughts like these?

- *How did she find a man to marry while I haven't? What does she have that I don't have?*
- *How did he get such a great job and I'm stuck in this boring one?*
- *She lost so much weight it makes her look older. Look how saggy her face is now!*
- *That new car he bought is really ostentatious. Where does he get the money for a car like that?*
- *She thinks she's the hottest thing going around here just because she got that employee-of-the-month award! Her job is a lot easier than mine!*

It's not always easy to rejoice with those who are rejoicing, is it?

Getting Rid of Jealousy

How do we motivate ourselves to want to rejoice with other people? It begins with digging out any jealousy that may arise over someone else's success. If you are not quick to rejoice at your coworker's good news, it is a warning of a wrong heart attitude within you.

The apostle Paul listed jealousy as one of the acts of the sinful nature (Gal 5:19-20), and Proverbs 27:4 says, "Anger is cruel and fury overwhelming, but who can stand before jealousy?" Who indeed? Jealousy can be more devastating than anger and fury, and it certainly can destroy relationships in quick order.

To keep jealousy out of your own heart, you need to recognize your wrong reactions toward the success of others, confess them as sin, and pray that God will deliver you from jealous feelings. If you have the new nature of a born-again person, you have the power to suffocate that old nature and keep the jealousy from ruling over you. But it won't happen without prayer and a willingness to change.

Think about this: A jealous heart is a sign of an insecure person. What I have discovered is that when I am growing in my Christian walk, when I allow the Word of God to convict and change me so that I am a maturing Christian (not a perfect one), and when that transformation process of 2 Corinthians 3:18 is evident in my life so that I am becoming more and more like Jesus, then I have less and less reason to be jealous of others. That's because I am more and more confident of who I am in Christ, what my calling is, how God sees me, and where my place is in his kingdom. This sets me free from comparing myself to others and allows me to rejoice at the good things that happen to others, or the success or gifts of others, without being jealous of them.

Rejoicing Suggestions

Here are some practical suggestions for rejoicing with someone on the job who has good news:

- Give a party to celebrate a friend's promotion or new job.
- Send a congratulatory note to someone for his or her significant accomplishment.
- Give or attend a shower—gladly, with gift in hand—to celebrate a baby on the way or an upcoming wedding.
- Take someone to dinner to celebrate good news from the doctor.
- Plan a celebration for a significant milestone in someone's life.

Hopefully you can add many other specifics to this list as you think about things that you have done, at your own instigation, to rejoice with someone. If you find it difficult to think of anything you've done, then perhaps that is sending you a message of an area that needs improvement.

Mourning With Others

The reason we may find it easier to mourn with those who have had some disappointment or tragedy in their lives is because we don't have to deal with the jealousy monster.

However, we still must be intentional about putting ourselves in the shoes of that person and taking part in his or her pain. That takes time and an abandonment of our own self-interests.

I find that it is difficult for me to mourn with someone who is mourning over something that I find insignificant or unworthy of mourning. If the problem is life-size, or if it is one not of that person's own doing, then I can usually "feel his or her pain" and join in their mourning. But when my judgmental spirit tells me that this person's mourning is foolish or childish, then I tend to ignore his or her pain.

I continually have to relearn this truth about relationships: we are not all in the same place at the same time, and what seems insignificant to me can be truly painful to someone else. True, it may be because that person is immature, but aren't we all at times? Haven't I been immature in the past and mourned over situations unworthy of such grief? Of course, but at the time it was very painful to me, even though it didn't rate higher than a 2 on a scale of 1 to 10!

I certainly think there are degrees of mourning, and we don't have to get mired in the pain of others when it is fairly inconsequential. But neither should we ignore it. It is painful to that person, and we should therefore recognize that pain.

Effective Mourning
It is very important to realize that the manner in which we mourn with others can be either positive or negative. You may have a sincere heart to share in someone's pain, but if you do so in the wrong way, you can make the pain worse.

One of my close friends lost her mother many years ago, and she called me at work to tell me. Though it was not unexpected, as her mother had been suffering with cancer for over a year, it was a terrible heartache. I knew at the first sound of her voice, before she could get the words out, what had happened, and I just said, "Oh, your mother's dead. I'm so sorry; I'm so sorry." I literally cried on the phone with her.

Later she told me how that had comforted her. Another dear friend, one who cared as much as I did about her loss, had said, "Now remember, your mother is in a better place and is no longer suffering. Don't cry; she's better off." All of that was true, of course, but it was of no comfort to my friend at that point in time. She didn't need to be told not to mourn; she needed someone to mourn with her.

I remember when a close friend at work was sharing a disappointment with a couple of us. We both just moaned and offered sympathy. "I'm so sorry; that's really rotten. You've sure had nothing but bad news lately, it seems." Do you know how she responded? She said, "Yes, but I know the Lord has a purpose in all this and we'll be OK."

I believe had either of us bombarded her with Scripture at that time, or tried to "cheer her up" by telling her it would be OK, it would have just caused her pain to increase. But because we mourned with her, she was able to remind herself of God's sovereignty, and that was a great comfort to her.

Job had friends who came to mourn with him, but they managed to lecture him as they mourned, explaining why he deserved to be suffering, giving their opinion of the cause of all his bad news.

After listening to their endless, self-righteous explanations, Job sarcastically expressed his feelings about the way they had "comforted" him: "How you have helped the powerless! How you have saved the arm that is feeble! What advice you have offered to one without wisdom! And what great insight you have displayed!" (Jb 26:2-3).

Can't you hear the sarcasm dripping from his lips? They came to mourn with him and ended up making him feel worse! They needed to learn how to mourn with those who mourn!

When coworkers have a grief or disappointment of some kind, don't give them clichés or advice. Don't quote Romans 8:28 to them, even if they are believers. Just mourn with them. That's what they need right then. You don't need great words of wisdom to help them cope. Your tears will do more than words will ever do.

Suggestions for Mourning With Others
Here are specific things we can do to mourn with someone who is mourning:

- Send a sympathy card when a loved one has died.
- Take food to someone who has become temporarily or permanently disabled.
- Cry with a friend over a broken relationship.
- Invite someone to be with you when you know that person is hurting over some rejection or feeling particularly alone.
- Give a hug or word of sympathy to someone who is hurting.
- Sit with a friend who is waiting for possible bad news or has already received it.
- Listen—a long time—to a friend pour out his or her heart to you about a painful experience.

You've probably done more of these things than you ever realized because, unfortunately, there always seems to be someone around us with a serious problem who needs a listening ear or a shoulder to cry on.

Personal Performance Review

Make a list of the things you have done in the last six months to rejoice with someone about his or her good news or success. (For example, giving a party to celebrate a friend's promotion, sending a congratulatory note to someone because of a significant accomplishment, taking someone out to eat to celebrate good news from the doctor.)

Then make a list of things you have done in the last six months to mourn with someone. (For example, sending a sympathy card, taking food to someone who has become disabled, giving a hug to someone who is hurting, sitting with a friend who is waiting for possible bad news, or listening—even a long time—to a friend pour out his or her heart about a painful experience.)

Chapter 4

Biblical Principle #4
Love Unconditionally

Two young men became fast friends. They were from different lifestyles—different "sides of the track," if you please. One was a humble shepherd; the other was the king's son, but they loved each other as though they were blood brothers.

Out of envy the king came to hate the shepherd and eventually schemed to kill him. But the king's son was very loyal to his friend and protected him from the king and his evil intentions, despite incurring the king's wrath and putting his own life at risk.

The shepherd boy was King David, and his friend was Jonathan, son of King Saul. Their friendship has become a symbol of devotion and unconditional love. Keep in mind that Jonathan was in line to take the throne, since he was the king's son, but God chose David instead. Yet Jonathan never let that interfere with their friendship. In fact, Jonathan said to David, "We have sworn friendship with each other in the name of the Lord" (1 Sm 20:42). Later David's own son gave us a beautiful description of this kind of friendship: "A friend loves at all times, and a brother is born for adversity" (Prv 17:17).

I've noticed that in interviews President George W. Bush

has repeatedly said about his relationship with his parents and their influence on his life, "They loved me unconditionally," and he describes their love as a major factor in his success as a person and a politician. Unconditional love, love that you know will be there for you no matter what, is powerful. It empowers people and motivates them as nothing else will.

After all, it is God's unconditional love for us that creates a desire in us to please him and keeps us in love with him. John wrote, "This is love: not that we loved God, but that he loved us and sent his Son as an atoning sacrifice for our sins" (1 Jn 4:10). Because God has so loved us, we are enticed to return that love, for love begets love.

Love at Work?

It may be true that you've never thought of many of your coworkers as friends that you love. You didn't choose them; they are just part of that job you go to each day. Many are not lovable; many have nothing in common with you; some may even be antagonistic. It just doesn't seem logical that loving unconditionally at all times would apply to those kinds of relationships, does it?

If we view love as something we give to those who love us, to those who induce us to love them by the way they treat us, then it would be true that we're not required to love some of the people on our jobs. But if we understand God's meaning of love, our conclusion would have to be different. According to John, "God is love. Whoever lives in love lives in God, and God in him" (1 Jn 4:16b). "Dear children, let us not love with words or tongue but with actions and in truth" (1 Jn 3:18).

This kind of love is an action, not a feeling. It is a decision, not a desire. Sometimes the feelings and desires are present; sometimes they are not. Either way, if we live in God, we must live in love. Therefore I conclude that we are to show friendship love through our attitudes and actions, even to those we have not personally chosen as our friends. That they are in our lives is enough. That is the God-thing to do, and it will take God's power to do it.

Loving at All Times

Loving unconditionally also means loving "at all times," and not just when everything's coming up roses and you've energy to burn. "All times" includes during your set-aside private time, in the middle of the night, or when you're tired or feeling very needy yourself, as well as when the other person isn't being very lovable, even when he or she is grumpy or has been taking advantage of you.

One of the greatest indications that we truly "live in God" and are new creations in Christ Jesus is our willingness to extend this God-love to people who would have no claim on our love otherwise. After all, your coworkers or boss or customers can't expect you to love them, can they? They can expect respect, civility, and perhaps sociability from us, but not love. It's not in your job description, and no one can demand it from you.

Therefore, when you choose to love in actions and truth, you show a loveless world a little sample of what Jesus is like.

You become the unconditional love of God reaching out to other persons. Its effect on the relationships of your life can be powerful.

Please don't confuse unconditional love with no-boundary love, however. We still need reasonable boundaries in all our relationships; love without boundaries can do more harm than good.

What Is Unconditional Love?

The famous love chapter in the Bible, 1 Corinthians 13, gives us a very practical description of what it means to love unconditionally. Here are just a few of the characteristics of love as given in that chapter.

Love Is Patient

Certainly you will be called on to exercise patience with the coworker who is slow to learn, your boss when he or she has unrealistic expectations, or a customer who blames you unfairly. Unconditional love will give you the ability to do that, rather than respond in anger or frustration.

Love Is Kind

Kind words are a choice you can make when responding to a rude person, a hurtful comment, an unfair accusation, or even a condescending coworker. When most people would respond with sarcasm or words that pierce like a sword, unconditional love gives you the power to speak gentle words that heal. Kindness is also something you can give to the coworker who is discouraged, the boss when he or she is grumpy, or an overly demanding customer. The person may not deserve it, and that makes it even more powerful when it is freely given.

Love Is Not Easily Angered

Unconditional love helps you avoid quick, defensive reactions. It gives you the power to control your hot temper. It enables you to resist the urge to shoot from the hip and give back a little of what you got. (Note that it does not say that love is never angered, just that it is not *easily* angered.)

Love Keeps No Record of Wrongs

It's funny how our memories work. We can forget birthdays and appointments but never forget how a coworker hurt our feelings last month or last year! Unconditional love does a lot of "erase disk" procedures, continually choosing to remove from the memory bank those wrongs done. It takes away our drive for revenge and leaves the revenge for God to handle. He tells us that revenge is his and he will repay (Rom 12:19), so there really is no need for us to keep a record of the wrongs done to us. They are God's responsibility, and he is far better at handling them than we are!

Love Does Not Delight in Evil but Rejoices With the Truth

This kind of unconditional love keeps you from spreading gossip. It eliminates the malicious talk that is so easy to participate in, especially when it is a common occurrence where you work. This love will make you seek the truth instead of believing everything you hear. It will make you suspicious of negative talk and bad reports.

Can you see how practical this principle is to our everyday lives? Loving with unconditional love—God's love—changes relationships because it changes our attitudes and actions. And it is a choice we make, not necessarily an emotion we feel.

My friend Beth worked at one time for a boss who was very condescending, very difficult to please, and demanding, even rude. This manager had not won many friends in the company, and yet Beth knew that God put this boss in her life for some good reason, so she began to pray for her. As Beth prayed for her, it changed Beth's own attitude and she began to see her boss differently.

Then Beth learned that the boss's birthday was coming up in a couple of weeks, and God gave her a strong nudge to buy her boss a birthday gift. This was not something that Beth would have chosen on her own to do. Gift-giving was not a common practice in the company, and doing it would not be comfortable for Beth, but she couldn't get away from that inner nudge.

Therefore in obedience she found an appropriate small gift and card. Then she thought, *What can I say in this card that I like about this boss?* She wanted to be complimentary but at the same time truthful. Beth realized that she could honestly say that she admired the boss's commitment to excellence and doing everything right, so in her note she thanked the boss for giving her a good example of striving for excellence.

When her boss's birthday rolled around, Beth placed the gift and card on her desk. She had no idea how this woman would respond, but she knew that God intended for her to give them to her. Later Beth's boss came to her with tears in her eyes, thanking her for her thoughtfulness. She was astonished that anyone would remember her birthday, and it marked a noticeable change in their relationship.

That was unconditional, unexpected love in action, and such love is virtually irresistible, even to the toughest heart.

Study Love

I have frequently challenged myself and others to read 1 Corinthians 13—a wonderful chapter—every day for a whole month. I encourage you to give it a try. It won't take more than five minutes each day, but it will really give you a very different perspective. God's definition of love is so totally opposite to the world's idea that we continually have to clean out our minds and get rid of all the wrong messages we've stored up, filling them up with God's truth instead.

One-Sided Relationships

A *one-sided relationship* is where one person gives and contributes to the relationship while the other simply takes.

Here's what Jesus had to say about these kinds of relationships:

If you love those who love you, what credit is that to you? Even "sinners" love those who love them. And if you do good to those who are good to you, what credit is that to you? Even "sinners" do that. And if you lend to those from whom you expect repayment, what credit is that to you? Even "sinners" lend to "sinners," expecting to be repaid in full.

LUKE 6:32-34

If you have any understanding of the culture in Jesus' day, you realize how absolutely outrageous this teaching was to the people who heard Jesus. No religion, no doctrine, no teacher, had ever dared to suggest that there was a responsibility to love people who don't love you! It was a concept most of them had never before considered. It was revolutionary.

And believe me, it is still revolutionary. Stop the average person on the street or in your company and ask, "Do you feel that you have a responsibility to love people who don't love you?" I can almost guarantee that you will get eight *nos* to every *yes*. If we practice this principle with the people on our job, therefore, it will have revolutionary results. It is behavior that cannot be explained in human terms. It is a God-thing.

One-Sided Work Relationships

Let me illustrate a hypothetical one-sided work relationship. Two nurses work together on the same shift. One nurse asks the other, whom she considers to be a good friend, to take some of the "dirty duty" for her. "Could you please just help me out this once?" is a phrase she uses frequently. Her "once" becomes a habit. Yet when asked to fill in on occasion for her "good friend," she never seems to find the time or to be available.

Do you have any one-sided relationships on your job? Here are some indications:

- Your coworker asks favors of you but is never willing to do anything for you.
- Your boss expects you to be available on short notice for overtime, extra work, and weekend work, but when you occasionally ask for some time off for needed personal business, he acts as though you are being unreasonable.
- Your friend bends your ear with every detail of her struggles at work but never has any interest in your job or struggles.
- Your coworker lets you pick up the tab for coffee, doughnuts, lunch, etc., but has never once offered to pay for yours.

Most people's response when they find themselves on the giving end of a one-sided relationship is to experience resentment, anger, withdrawal, bitterness, or a desire for getting even. These are understandable emotions, and most people would not blame them.

But what is not understandable is a response of unconditional love. The only explanation for it is that the love of God compels you, and you are willing to allow his love to flow from him through you to the person on the receiving end of your one-sided relationship. Where others would shift blame and decide that they owe nothing to this "taker" person, you continue to treat him or her with kindness, respect, and unexpected, undeserved mercy and generosity.

Unconditional love is not enabling love. One thing you need to watch for in these one-sided relationships is the tendency to become an enabler. An enabler is one who allows a person to take advantage of him or her, refuses to confront appropriately, and thereby allows that person to prolong his or her poor behavior and reinforces his or her bad habits.

I remember a letter from a woman telling me how her boss and coworkers were taking advantage of her. The boss gave her extra work and the work others didn't want to do because he knew she would do it and do it well. Her coworkers actually made fun of her for being a "patsy," and they never included her in their lunch invitations. So she became a loner and the workhorse for the office with nothing to show for it!

A nurse wrote to me about her situation. She loved her job, but somehow without realizing it, she had taken on more responsibility in the hospital than the other nurses had. She was a "go-to" person, and "go-to" people are quick to get the job done, know how to make things work, aren't afraid to try anything, and actually enjoy being a "go-to" person. That's why people "go to" them. However, this nurse had not learned where to draw the line, and she was facing burnout and exhaustion.

Without realizing it, both of these women had become enablers. Because they continually stepped in and picked up the slack, others were able to avoid their duties and responsibilities. They were (maybe still are!) reinforcing bad habits.

If you recognize any enabling tendencies in yourself, you need to take seriously the boundary-setting suggestions in chapter one. You'll find it difficult to withdraw from being an enabler because you'll feel guilty at first. Many enablers are guilt-motivated—motivated by false guilt, that is. But you can change, and it will benefit not only you but the ones you are enabling as well.

It is well to remember, however, that all relationships go through cycles, so don't give up on a relationship where you may be doing all the giving for a while. Certainly as parents we have years of this with our children; it is our job as parents to give more than we receive. Actually, part of the joy of parenting is to be able to give even though our children don't give back in return.

Love Never Fails

Paul wrote that simple sentence to the Corinthians (1 Cor 13:6a), and I remember memorizing that chapter as a young girl in Sunday school. "Love never fails." It sounds so poetic, so idealistic, so right, but it is far more than just beautiful words. It is a great and powerful truth.

Is there anything else you can identify that never fails, besides God? Money fails; the stock market fails; success fails; people fail; your health fails! But love never fails!

That means that when you show love toward someone, it never fails to reach him or her. When you act in loving ways toward a person, even an unlovable person, it will never fail to make a difference. When you choose to love a coworker, it will never fail to improve that relationship.

Love never fails. When you don't know what else to do, love. When everything else has failed, love. When a person looks like a hopeless case, love. Choose to love in spite of your feelings. Choose to love regardless of whether it is received well or not. Choose to love even if your love is never reciprocated. Love never fails.

Loving others is always guaranteed to change you, even if you never see any change in the other person. When you choose to replace resentment and frustration with love, you will see tremendous improvements in yourself. As a rule, those improvements will make a difference in the other person, but even if they don't, you cannot lose because love never fails.

I can promise you that love never fails because God's Word says so. Therefore I am absolutely certain that if you show unconditional love toward those people you have not heretofore loved, those people who make your life more difficult, those people who don't deserve your love, it will not fail. It will succeed. Good things will happen.

And the joy you are going to discover because of your obedience to God will amaze you. It really is awesome to see God do in you what you cannot do in yourself. You're in for some great adventures and marvelous results.

Personal Performance Review

It might be helpful to do a quick survey of the people you are most closely associated with on your job and to evaluate your own attitude toward each of them. Give it a try!

Divide a piece of paper into three vertical columns. In the first (left) column, write the names of people with whom you relate at work.

Now move to the middle column. Next to each name write a word or phrase that describes how you feel about that person (for example, loving, resentful, neutral, admiring).

Third, look over the names and the feeling descriptions you

have written. If you have indicated some nonloving attitudes toward any of these people, ask yourself, "Am I willing to pray that God will love them through me?" Write your answer in the third column. (Remember that it is his love flowing through you to them. And remember too, love is not necessarily a feeling; it is a choice.)

If you have answered, "No, not yet," across from any of the names, don't give up! God can change your "wanter"! Keep praying about it.

If yes is your answer, I encourage you to put a love action plan in writing and become very intentional about showing love to those unlovable people.

My Love Action Plan

On a clean sheet of paper, list the people you are willing to let God love through you. Leave plenty of space after each name.

Then go back over the list and identify a specific love action that you could do within the next week to ten days. You will be able to think of others, but here are some examples to get you started. Pray that God will show you the best love action for each person.

- invite him [her] to lunch
- listen to her [him] talk
- speak with kind words and tone
- send a congratulatory card or e-mail
- ask him [her] for advice
- offer to help with workload

- smile at her [him]
- compliment him [her]
- bake or buy goodies and share
- do some "dirty work" for her [him]

After a couple of weeks, when you have completed your "love actions," come back to your list and note the changes you have seen in the other person, if any. Then note the changes you have seen in yourself.

Chapter 5

Biblical Principle #5
Be a Good Listener

Jesus invited three of his closest disciples to take a hike with him to a high mountain. When they arrived, these three guys saw something they had never seen before: Jesus was changed right in front of their eyes, and all of a sudden Moses and Elijah were right there on that mountain, too, talking to Jesus. It was awesome!

One of these disciples was so excited and so frightened that he didn't know what to say. So he started to talk. At a time when he needed to keep his mouth shut and listen, he talked. In the midst of his nervous and excited babbling, God spoke directly from heaven to him, saying, "This is my Son, whom I love. Listen to him!" (Mk 9:7b).

Peter definitely needed to learn how to listen. He was a talker, a doer, and a leader. It must have blown his mind to hear God telling him to *listen!*

God's Word speaks the same message to us today, just as powerfully as he did to Peter on the Mount of Transfiguration. And he urges us to be good listeners. As James put it, "Everyone should be quick to listen, slow to speak and slow to become angry" (Jas 1:19b).

71

The Importance of Listening

When was the last time you said or thought, "You know, the problem with that person is he [she] just doesn't listen"? It's a fairly common complaint in relationships, and it can cause hard feelings and distance between people. When someone refuses to listen to us, especially if it represents a pattern in that relationship, we feel undervalued, perhaps even rejected—certainly not appreciated.

Obviously, if it's important that others listen to us, it is equally important that we learn to listen to others. Some people are just naturally good listeners. Others find it is a skill that has to be acquired. But whether you find it easy or not, it is incumbent on each of us to work seriously at improving our listening skills. You've noticed that God gave us two ears and one mouth. Could it be a hint as to the appropriate balance between how much we should talk and how much we should listen?

Too Much Talk

Suppose you could record all your words for a typical day. When you analyzed the tape, which would you find: more time speaking or more time listening? Until we learn to practice the principle of being slow to speak, we probably won't be very good listeners; you can't listen while you're talking.

Think of someone you know who talks too much. Does that bad habit not cause some relationship problems, with you and others? It really is smart to go easy with your words. Even if your words are harmless, when you talk too much you cause people not to want to be around you.

Besides, if you talk a lot you're bound to say something you shouldn't. Proverbs 10:19 warns us, "When words are many, sin is not absent, but he who holds his tongue is wise." Solomon also gave us some further good advice when he wrote, "He who answers before listening—that is his folly and his shame" (Prv 18:13).

To refuse to listen to someone, to respond before truly hearing a person out, is folly. That means it's foolish, absurd, unwise; could we even say stupid? Remember that we never learn anything as long as we are talking. A wise person knows the importance of developing good listening habits. As you become a better listener, it is guaranteed to improve every relationship in your life.

Improving Your Listening Skills

Since I am not naturally a good listener, it didn't take me long to recognize where my weaknesses were once I began to give it some thought. However, I went many years before even thinking about whether I was a good listener or not, and so my bad listening habits were allowed to continue and get worse.

Yet since I began thinking and praying about my poor listening habits many years ago, I have become acutely aware of my areas of weakness. Unfortunately there are quite a few, but there is no doubt that God has enabled me to improve in those areas, and though he's not finished with me yet, I'm a better listener than I used to be.

Identifying Weaknesses

To begin improving our listening skills, we must first identify where we are failing. A person may not even realize that his or her listening skills are weak. Yet poor listening can be a major hindrance in relationships, so it's worthwhile to seriously evaluate them.

One way to start is to ask a few close friends, coworkers, or family members, or if you are married, your mate and your children. Give them permission to critique your listening skills and advise you on where your listening weaknesses might be.

If you are honest with yourself, you'll be able to learn quite a bit on your own. Start by seeing if any of the following describe you.

- I am often thinking of what I am going to say instead of really listening.
- My mind wanders easily, and I think about other things while another person is speaking.
- I tend to interrupt people.
- I often complete other people's sentences for them.
- I do other things when someone is talking to me and become distracted instead of listening.
- I'm always correcting people when they talk to me.
- I allow my prejudices to influence what I hear, and I make judgments while listening.
- I am a selective listener, hearing what interests or pleases me and screening out what I consider unimportant or unpleasant.

Replacing Bad Habits With Good Ones

Once you identify your bad listening habits, start working on them one at a time. Each day pray about a specific bad habit, asking God to help you remember to be a better listener and not to ... [name the problem behavior]. Calling it by name every day before God will cause you to become more and more aware of your listening failures. This is absolutely essential if you want to change. You cannot do it without God's power and God's motivation, and those come through daily bringing your problem before him in prayer.

You'll also want to start replacing your bad listening habits with good ones. Here are some very practical ways to do that.

You often think of what you are going to say next instead of listening. I frequently find myself doing this, and I really have to work hard at reminding myself to listen instead of formulating my next speech. I began to be motivated to change this bad habit when I realized it was arrogance and pride on my part to think that what I had to say was more important than what the other person was saying.

I also recognized that part of my listening problem is my lack of patience. If someone is not talking as quickly as I would like, or they don't get to the point in an efficient way, I begin to tune them out.

There is no magic dust to rid you of this bad habit. You do it by self-control and praying about it every day. Thus you become aware when you are doing it and learn to refocus your mind and make yourself listen to the other person. One other thing that does help is to look the other person straight in the eye as he or she talks.

It takes an intentional set of your will, but you can learn just to concentrate on what the other person is saying to you rather than thinking of what you're going to say next.

Your mind wanders while others talk. I confess that this is another one of my bad habits. I find myself thinking about all kinds of other things instead of listening. I can give good listening signals, like good eye contact and nodding my head, yet never really hear what the other person is saying to me because my mind wanders off so easily.

One way to help yourself concentrate is to take notes while you're listening. I have found this to be especially helpful when I'm on the phone. Another strategy is to look into someone's eyes and tell yourself, *Listen!* while that person is talking to you. I find that I have to repeatedly bring myself up short with mental reminders to stay focused, but as you begin to exercise more self-control, you will find that you gradually are listening better.

You tend to interrupt people or complete their sentences for them. These are very irritating habits. If you do either thing often, I can assure you that it is creating some communication problems for you with others. Interrupting people when they're talking certainly doesn't show an attitude of caring, and it is truly bad manners.

In order to stop this behavior, you're going to need some outside help. Chances are you don't even realize you're doing it, so ask the people close to you to help by calling it to your attention. If you give them permission to point out your interruptions, you won't get irritated with them for doing it.

Imagine a coworker who kindly says to you, "Excuse me, Mary, you interrupted me again," and suppose that happens four times in one hour. Do you think you'd start to become more and more sensitive to this bad habit? It definitely will work, but you have to have the courage and the willingness to have this bad habit exposed.

Let me assure you that this will definitely improve your relationships, even though it may be uncomfortable for a few days. Not only will you begin to break this bad listening habit, but your coworker will truly appreciate and admire your willingness to change. Who knows? Maybe it will help others to recognize their need to change in this area as well.

You do other things while others are talking and become distracted. I'll never forget when a good friend pointed out to me that I tended to do other things while talking with her on the telephone. She told me it really offended her. I was shocked because I thought she would understand my need to get things done, even while we were talking. After all, I'm a busy person!

Do you hear the arrogance in that line of thinking? I didn't until she made me aware of this bad listening habit. She could hear me rustling papers or working at the computer while we talked, and I'm sure that even though I thought I could do two things at once, it was obvious that I was not hearing everything she said. And my behavior was telling her that she was not important enough for me to put aside other work for our conversation.

This bad habit is possible in face-to-face conversations as well as those on the telephone. Lack of eye contact, shifting in your seat a lot, uneasiness in your body language—these tend to send similar messages, demonstrating distraction on your part and greatly hindering effective communication.

I now try to make myself stop what I'm doing when I talk with someone, on the phone or in person. Turning away from the computer, pushing away what you are reading, leaning toward the person who is talking to you, giving good eye contact—all of these eliminate distractions and help you focus on what the other person is saying.

You're always correcting people when they talk. You allow your prejudices to influence what you hear. You make judgments while listening. You are a selective listener, hearing what interests or pleases you and screening out what you consider unimportant or unpleasant. These bad listening habits all have deep roots in our hearts and require some real soul-searching for us to change them.

Correcting people is evidence of a judgmental heart. It comes from looking for what someone is saying that is wrong and pouncing on it, instead of truly listening to hear and understand what they are saying and where they are coming from. It indicates an attitude of "I'm always right."

Prejudicial listening happens when we judge books by their covers and relegate people to certain categories, based on our prejudices, before we hear what they have to say. That prejudice could be the way a person dresses, a person's race or color, a person's economic status or educational level—prejudice comes in many forms, and all of us tend to have some of it lurking in our hearts. We look on the outside, but God looks on the heart, so we need to listen to that person as an individual, without our own biases.

Selective listeners are those who choose to hear only what they want to hear. These are people who are adverse to change, cannot confront their own failures, or are never willing to hear anyone else's point of view. Parents of teenagers are often familiar with this bad habit, but it is certainly not limited to that one age group.

Can you see how these attitudes will not only keep you from being an effective listener but profoundly damage relationships? They need to be recognized, confessed, and prayed out of our lives.

One way to attack these bad habits is to force yourself to paraphrase back to the other person what you just heard him or her say, before reacting or responding in any way. Paraphrasing is repeating what you heard but in your own words. If you say to me, "Now, if I understand you correctly ..." and proceed to paraphrase what I've said, then I know both that you're listening and that you care enough to make sure you heard correctly. It will also help to eliminate your prejudice, tendency to correct, and selective listening habits.

The Benefits of Good Listening

As you begin to be a better listener, you'll notice some improvements in you and in your relationships.

- You won't jump to wrong conclusions so often.
- You won't say something you regret so frequently.
- You'll learn a lot about your coworkers and get to know them better.

- Your stress will be reduced.
- Morale will improve.
- Your attitude will be more positive.
- Communication will greatly improve.
- You'll make fewer mistakes.
- You'll have fewer misunderstandings.
- You'll be more productive.
- Getting up and going to work won't be so hard!

Imagine all that is possible if we are willing to work at being better listeners. Those are powerful benefits, and it is within our power to make them happen.

However, the most important motivation to be a better listener is because we want to live in obedience to our Lord and Savior, to live by biblical standards and principles. I find that when nothing else can motivate me to change, I am always motivated by a desire to please the one who loved me and gave himself for me. And the incredible truth is that he will work this miracle of change in us if we are willing to let him do it.

Personal Performance Review

Review the list of statements in the section of this chapter entitled "Improving Your Listening Skills." Write down those that sound like you.

If you select more than two, choose the top two that you feel need immediate attention. Then identify one or two remedies, or strategies, that would help you replace the bad listening habit with a good one. If you need help getting started in finding remedies, review the discussion in the section of this chapter entitled "Replacing Bad Habits With Good Ones."

Remember, you won't change overnight, but you will change if you pray about it and tackle one or two bad habits at a time. If you find that your listening skills are really in bad shape, like mine were, please don't be discouraged. When you see a change in one bad habit, it will encourage you to keep on until they are all changed.

Chapter 6

Biblical Principle #6

Be Dependable and Loyal

A young man, who was greatly influenced by his godly mother and grandmother, made a choice early in his life to be a helper to the great apostle Paul. He became Paul's most dependable and loyal assistant. All through Paul's letters to the various churches you will find references to Timothy. Many times when he was not able to go himself, Paul sent Timothy to encourage and help the churches.

Paul valued Timothy immensely. In fact, he considered him a son in the Lord. And the reason this young man was of such value in God's service was because he was faithful and loyal. (See 1 Cor 4:17.)

Young Timothy had attributes that are invaluable to any leader, manager, company, or individual. You've heard the cliché, "The best ability is dependability." It's far more than a cliché. It is truth! Paul wrote to the Philippians, "I have no one else like [Timothy], who takes a genuine interest in your welfare.... But you know that Timothy has proved himself, because as a son with his father he has served with me in the work of the gospel" (Phil 2:20, 22).

I remember when, early in my sales career, my boss promised

me a promotion if I sold a certain quota. I worked my head off to reach that goal—and it wasn't easy. Naturally I was very pleased when I made the deadline and could proudly walk into my boss's office, show him my sales record, and receive my promised reward.

I'll never forget the sheepish look on his face and his stammering response to me. He certainly was pleased about my sales accomplishments, but he had to tell me that he had made a promise to me he could not keep. Evidently his boss had informed him that he didn't have the authority to give me that promotion, and even though I came through on my end, he was not able to come through on his.

He did apologize, and I tried to let it go, but it affected our relationship from then on. First, I no longer could fully believe him when he promised something. Second, it affected my respect for his position, as I realized he didn't have the authority or power I had thought he had. Third, he was a bit uneasy with me for a long time afterward; that broken promise hung between us like a black cloud. Broken promises have that kind of effect on relationships.

What Is Your Dependability Reputation?

Did you realize that you have a dependability reputation? The people who work with you see you as very dependable, sometimes dependable, or undependable. A reputation for dependability takes a long time to build, but it can be torn down very quickly. And your dependability reputation affects your relationships dramatically.

I can think of people from whom I have distanced myself

because I have learned that they are not dependable. They are often very vocal about what they will do, but they don't show up! They've left me holding the bag, disappointed because they promised but did not deliver. As a result, my respect for them has been damaged, and while I may like them personally, I simply don't want to be involved in any kind of a project with them because they've proven undependable.

When coworkers prove undependable, I may have to pick up the pieces after them many times. That means I may miss important deadlines and commitments because they dropped the ball. It means last-minute crises, poor work product, disappointed customers, egg on my face, embarrassed explanations or excuses, ad infinitum. So, though I still want to treat them with kindness, I really don't want to work with them. Their lack of dependability represents trouble.

Some of the people in my life are very dependable. Those people are the ones I want on my team. They are trustworthy; I love working with them; I enjoy partnering with them in any way. The relationship is a comfortable one, a trusting one, and therefore an enjoyable one. The respect we share for each other is significant.

Dependability definitely enhances relationships. This is a strong biblical principle, and I really want to urge you to become very serious about being a dependable person.

The Consequences of Broken Promises

Solomon understood how devastating broken promises could be. He wrote, "Hope deferred makes the heart sick, but a longing fulfilled is a tree of life" (Prv 13:12).

"Hope deferred" is another way of describing disappointment. Any time you make a promise or a commitment to someone, you build hope in that person. He or she is hopeful that you will do what you've said you would do. If you fail to keep that promise without a very good reason or explanation, it does something to that person's heart—to his or her feelings toward you. That deferred hope—that unfulfilled promise—makes the heart sick, as wise Solomon said it would.

Think of the residual effects of a broken promise, a missed commitment, or a failed follow-through. They vary, of course, with the severity of the situation and the people involved. But you can be certain that there are residual effects. They could include some or all of the following:

- disappointment
- anger
- feelings of rejection
- destroyed trust
- estrangement
- poor job performance
- poor evaluation
- loss of raise or promotion
- loss of respect
- loss of confidence

It changes your feelings toward a person when you recognize that they are not dependable. Obviously a one-time failure should not cause permanent damage, and we all need to give people second and third chances. Certainly we need that kind of compassion and consideration at times ourselves, because none of us has a perfect track record of being totally dependable. However, if there is a person who is frequently undependable, it makes for a difficult relationship.

Under-Promise; Over-Deliver

Ecclesiastes 5:5 says, "It is better not to vow than to make a vow and not fulfill it." Solomon again gives us great advice here concerning making promises and commitments.

A great little motto to remember is "Under-promise; over-deliver." Be careful that you don't glibly promise what you can't or don't intend to fulfill. Think carefully about your commitments. It is better not to vow at all than to fail to keep a vow, and it makes a great impression if you come through with more than you promised or sooner than you promised. That's a lot easier to explain than missing the mark!

Dependability Evaluation

What would your answers have to be to the following questions?

- Do my coworkers consider me to be very dependable?
- Am I usually on time for appointments?
- Do I often miss deadlines?
- Am I careless about keeping track of what I'm supposed to do and when I'm supposed to do it?
- Do I make unrealistic promises under pressure too easily?

Assuming that dependability is not your strongest suit, I encourage you to dig deep and ask yourself why you have developed this bad habit of being undependable, of breaking promises. Here are some possibilities; see if any of them fit.

- The role models of my life (parents, family, friends) are not very dependable.
- I have a lazy streak that creates a lack of dependability in me.
- I have very good intentions, but my lack of organizational skills causes me to be undependable.
- I am a very poor time manager and tend to be a procrastinator, which leads to lack of dependability.
- I get distracted easily and forget my promises and commitments frequently.
- I do not have enough self-control or discipline in my own personal habits.
- I frequently make promises that are unrealistic.

Improving Your Dependability

Step one in making improvements is identifying our weaknesses. If you are able to identify any of the statements you just read as factors in your own lack of dependability, you've made that important first step. Now you are poised to make some changes.

List your areas of frequent failure in your prayer journal, and begin praying about them daily. As a believer you have an incredible power source in the Holy Spirit, who dwells within you and allows you to change.

But that change has to begin with a motivation to change, in order to please the Lord, and then an intentional effort on your part to make specific changes. Here are some suggestions to help you incorporate needed change.

Find Role Models

My parents taught my brothers and me dependability by their example. They were always on time, usually early. They took every promise as a test of their "word," and their "word" was good. Dependability was expected in our home, and I grew up thinking everybody had that same characteristic built into them as I had. I've learned that is not the case, and I recognize the value of my role models to me. I have such a lazy streak in me that I doubt I would be a dependable person if I had not had such good upbringing.

If you were not raised with good role models, it will make change more challenging but not impossible. Ask God to give you some substitute role models. Find people you know who are what you want to be and watch them. Follow in their steps. Not having early role models does not have to handicap you for life.

Remember, you are role modeling for someone else: children, coworkers, friends. Even if you didn't have the role models you needed, you can break that chain and not inflict the same disadvantage on those who look to you for examples of dependability.

Face that Lazy Streak

In the parable of the talents, Jesus tells what happens to the lazy servant, the one who refused to multiply his talent. The master says to this servant, "You wicked, lazy servant! So you knew that I harvest where I have not sown and gather where I have not scattered seed? Well, then, you should have put my money on deposit with the bankers, so that when I returned I would have received it back with interest. Take the talent from him and give it to the one who has ten talents" (Mt 25:26-28).

"Wicked" and "lazy" are strong accusations, and all this poor guy did was to do nothing! Laziness is not a little problem we may have; it is a sin. God doesn't find it amusing or acceptable.

Your first step in overcoming your lazy streak is to call it what it is: a sin in God's eyes. Start praying about that lazy streak each day, recognizing how God sees it. Throughout your day remind yourself of how God views laziness. Get serious about attacking this bad habit.

Do What You Don't Want to Do First!

One suggestion that I find very helpful: Do your unpleasant tasks first. Get them behind you early in the day, and you will be amazed at how energized you are once those things are behind you. This will truly help those who tend to procrastinate, too. Frankly, it's a gimmick I use on myself all the time, so I can assure you it really helps.

Acquire a Daily Planning System

It's true that some people are more naturally organized than others, but all of us need enough organizational skills to keep track of what we are supposed to do and when. There really is no excuse for us in this area, because we have so many options and helps available to us. If this tends to be your problem, you need to find the daily planning system that works for you and make yourself use it faithfully. It could be as simple as a to-do list on a legal pad or a carefully kept calendar or as sophisticated as a Palm Pilot, but you have to use it daily and faithfully. Libraries are full of how-to books on time management. Seminars on the topic proliferate. This is not a difficult area in which to find help, but you have to do it. Nobody is going to do it for you.

Uncover Your Hidden Causes for Unrealistic Promises
Many times we set ourselves up for failure by making promises that are unrealistic. If this is one of your problems, ask yourself why you tend to over-promise. Is it to win friends and influence people? Is it to avoid an unpleasant situation at the moment? Is it because you try to please everyone? Is it because you don't think before you promise? Investigate it, and determine why you have that tendency. Then make it a matter of daily prayer.

Every time you start to say yes, stop and ask yourself if this is a realistic commitment. Ask yourself if this is a boundary issue (see chapter one). Are you trying to be all things to all people? Make yourself think before you commit.

Buy yourself some time by saying something like, "Let me think about that a minute"—or a day or a week! If you forget and make a commitment too quickly, go back as soon as you can and withdraw the commitment. That won't be easy, but if done quickly enough, it is much better than making foolish promises. You can say something like, "You know, I spoke too quickly, which is one of my bad habits. I need to think about this before I say yes. I want to be sure I can deliver what I promise, so let me get back with you on this."

The Loyalty Component

In the same way that you have a dependability reputation, you also have a track record and a reputation for loyalty. We associate loyalty with our close friends and family, but there is definitely a loyalty component in our work relationships as well.

Disloyalty and Its Consequences

Consider these scenarios and their likely consequences.

You have a coworker with whom you've worked for some time. She and you have shared many personal matters in confidence, and you have come to trust her. Then you discover that she has been relating your personal confidences to other people. Potential consequences:

- You are deeply hurt by the betrayal of your trust, and that pain will affect the way you communicate, the commitment you have to the relationship, and your willingness to extend yourself to that coworker.
- You are not likely to share any confidences with this person again.
- You become suspicious of this person's ability to be trusted in other areas.

Your coworker pretends to be your friend when he's with you, but behind your back he makes fun of you, tells things that are not true about you, and tries to create strife between you and others on the job. Potential consequences:

- You are angered by the hypocrisy of this coworker. That anger could exhibit itself in words, body language, withdrawal, or any number of other negative ways on your part.
- You disassociate yourself from this coworker.

Your boss failed to stand up for you and the others in your department when you were falsely accused of a mistake. Potential consequences:
- Your trust in your boss has been damaged.
- Your willingness to "stick your neck out" for the boss or the company has been eliminated.
- Your loyalty to the boss is diminished.

Your coworker takes credit for what you have done, or your boss does not give you credit for what you have accomplished. Potential consequences:
- You feel resentment or anger because you have been cheated out of what was rightfully yours.
- Your relationship takes on a much more cautious tone and is cold, at best.

These are some common examples of lack of loyalty in work relationships, and I'm sure you've experienced one or more along the way. In each situation, think of the damage done to those relationships by the lack of loyalty that was demonstrated.

This is not to say that apologies, confrontations, and forgiveness cannot remedy mistakes made in relationships. These are always essential in good relationships, because all of us will fail and need restoration. (See chapter nine.) However, preventative measures are far wiser than rehabilitation, and it is true that some relationship damages leave scars that never are erased entirely. That is particularly true when it comes to loss of trust.

Loyalty Has a Lot to Do With the Tongue!
You've undoubtedly noticed by now that I have many references to Solomon. That's because the Book of Proverbs (and

Ecclesiastes) is chock-full of great advice and foundational principles that are essential for good relationships. Solomon wasn't considered the wisest man who ever lived without good reason! And again he gives us a revealing glimpse of what loyalty is all about when he says, "He who covers over an offense promotes love, but whoever repeats the matter separates close friends" (Prv 17:9).

A loyal person will protect a relationship—defend it if necessary. Loyalty requires me to be on guard against anything harmful to my friend, coworker, boss, or company. Loyalty causes me to downplay any problem or offense any of them might commit. Loyalty eliminates gossip and backbiting and a critical spirit. Loyalty causes me to stand up for the relationship, even if it threatens harm to myself.

Loyalty Versus Cover-Up

Remember, loyalty will cover over an offense, but that doesn't mean you whitewash sin. We need to be clear in any relationship that we never condone wrong behavior and are never willing to cover up what should be exposed and corrected. But if I am trying to protect a relationship, I will never be part of the gossip and maligning that so often occur. Furthermore, if there is a situation that needs to be exposed, a loyal person will do so very cautiously, going first to the individual involved and exercising every precaution to control the damage.

Loyal friends do everything they can to keep down the rumors, to keep from exposing their friends or coworkers to criticism or embarrassment. They try to deal with a situation in a quiet way, keeping it out of the public eye if possible.

Recently a good friend shared with me a painful family

situation involving one of her children. Then she told me that she and her husband have decided to keep this quiet except among a very few close friends and family, in order to protect her child from further embarrassment. That is a very wise decision because she wants to give this child as much cover as possible in anticipation of the day when this is part of the past, as we all pray it will be soon.

Loyal people are not eager to pass along something offensive about a friend or coworker. Just the opposite, they seek to protect that relationship, and they hang in there with that person as long as they can without compromising their own beliefs or testimony.

The Evil of Gossip

Solomon says, "Whoever repeats the matter separates close friends" (Prv 17:9). "Repeats the matter" is another way of saying "gossip," and gossip is always harmful to relationships. It doesn't bring people together; it separates them.

The Bible has a great deal to say about the sin of gossip. And remember, it is a sin even if it is true. If we gossip about others, passing on derogatory information that is neither lovely nor necessary, we damage the relationship we have with that person and the relationships they have with others. Gossip is one of the major factors in broken relationships.

I am convinced that we're all far more prone to gossip than we realize. I urge you to become very aware of gossip—saying or listening to something about a person which is not complimentary and not necessary to say. It displays a real lack of loyalty, and the damage done has a ripple effect far beyond the immediate reaction.

I have been privileged to minister at the Brooklyn Tabernacle and attend some of their services. Twice I have heard Pastor Cymbala give an official welcome to new members. Each time, with the new members standing at the front of his church, he has taken about ten minutes to tell them the church's position on gossip.

He tells them that gossip is not allowed in this church. (It shouldn't be allowed in any church, should it?) He says, "If someone comes to you and says anything negative about me or any other staff member or any church member, you are to stop them right away and say, 'Have you gone to Pastor Cymbala?' or whomever they are talking about. If they have not, you are to say, 'Let's go right now. I will go with you, and we will get this matter settled right away.'"

Gossip is one of the most destructive forces in a church congregation, in a family, or in a company. We really must recognize our responsibility to be loyal to the relationships of our lives and have no part of any kind of gossip. I urge you to put Pastor Cymbala's instructions in place in your own life.

Personal Performance Evaluation

Look back at the questions that were posed in this chapter under the title "Dependability Evaluation." Make a list of any areas of weakness you can identify in yourself.

Then ask some people you work with how they view you regarding dependability and loyalty. (By the way, when you ask someone for an honest critique, it always comes in a much more palatable form than when it is given in anger or frustration. So, buck up and ask, "How am I doing?")

If you are very dependable and loyal, you'll get some good comments that will encourage you. If you are somewhat dependable and loyal, you'll get some hedging in their comments. If you are undependable or disloyal, they may be forthright in telling you or simply try to avoid answering you. But one way or the other, it will give you some very good constructive feedback.

Add to your list anything new you may have learned from your friends or coworkers. Then study the list and underscore your two worst habits or tendencies that cause you to be undependable or disloyal.

Once you do this, the hard part is behind you. Now begin a prayer campaign about the things on your list. One by one, work at changing those bad habits. You will be excited and encouraged to see that, with God's help, you *can* change.

Chapter 7

Biblical Principle #7
Confronting Constructively

A great leader had a great moral failure. He had not only disgraced himself and his country, but he disgraced the name of God Almighty, whom he professed to serve.

The Lord sent his prophet to confront this king. To help him see how terrible was his sin, the prophet told the king a simple story of how a rich man betrayed a poor man. The king was furious as he heard of how the rich man acted. Then the prophet said to him, "You are the man!" And with that, the prophet confronted the king in no uncertain terms, outlining exactly how he had done evil in the eyes of the Lord and explaining the heavy price he would have to pay. To the king's credit, he immediately accepted his responsibility and admitted, "I have sinned against the Lord."

You, of course, recognize the biblical story of the confrontation between the prophet Nathan and King David (2 Samuel 12:1-14). This was a situation in which confrontation was absolutely needed and God-directed. The need arises in our world today, as well. Whether the concern is a major moral issue or simply the more common daily offenses that crop up, there are times when we, like Nathan, need to confront someone, even on our jobs.

However, I think if we took a survey of the things we don't like to do, confrontation would come out somewhere near the top. Whether on the job or in our personal lives, most of us struggle with how and when to confront someone. It is not a pleasant experience and is one we often avoid or postpone. Yet confrontation can be one of the most constructive things we can do to improve our relationships—when it is done at the right time, for the right reason, and in the right way.

In this chapter we are going to demonstrate the consequences of failure to confront when you need to, the potential benefits of constructive confrontation, and most importantly, the guidelines you need to follow when it is right for you to confront. This is one of the most important lessons to learn in developing your ability to improve your relationships.

Avoiding Confrontation

When we avoid confrontation where it is needed, we usually cause further damage.

The Consequences of Avoiding Confrontation

Consider this hypothetical scenario:

You and I work together as peers, but I have been on the job longer than you have. Your work habits have become a constant source of frustration to me because you don't do your work carefully and your many errors end up on my desk and cause me considerably extra work.

As a result this has boiled up inside of me until I feel

very put upon, and I share my frustration with another coworker, who is a good friend of mine. In other words, I go into gossip mode and tell this other coworker what I don't like about you, etc., etc. Since this other person is a friend of mine, she is influenced by what I've told her about you.

Shortly thereafter my good friend is having a conversation with another coworker in another part of the company. Your name surfaces innocently, and my friend passes on the negative report about you that she has heard from me. Before long this gossip has spread through the company, and your reputation is damaged.

You notice a change in the way some coworkers interact with you and sense something has happened, but you have no idea what it is. You just know that it's not much fun to work here any longer because of the poor working relationships that have developed.

In this hypothetical situation, you would now encounter relationship problems with your coworkers because of my gossip. Consider other possible consequences:

- Company morale suffers.
- You develop ulcers!
- Your attitude takes a turn downward.
- Productivity is down; wasted time is up.
- Inaccurate work continues, affecting customers adversely.
- The boss is not happy.
- I continue to be frustrated over your poor work habits, and that affects my attitude even more.

You get the point. Now here's the next important consideration. What other choices did I have in responding to your poor work habits, and what effect would each of them been likely to have?

I could have gone to the boss and complained about you, hoping the boss would correct you and solve the problem. Complaining to the boss without first trying to resolve the issue with you would have made me look like a snitch. Furthermore, once you found out, our relationship would have had little hope of ever improving.

I could have said and done nothing, hoping the problem would just go away. Keeping my mouth closed and doing nothing would have surely led to bitterness and anger on my part, which eventually would have come out in an uncontrolled, destructive way.

I could have confronted you constructively, without talking to anyone else. This is the only option that really makes sense. If this road had been taken, it is likely we would have resolved the matter satisfactorily, just between us.

Our Reluctance to Confront
Do any of the following statements sound like you?

- I rarely confront anyone about anything because it is very uncomfortable and I try to avoid anything unpleasant.
- I fear the reaction from the person I need to confront,

and I don't want to hurt his or her feelings, so I'm very reluctant to confront.

- I feel so guilty about myself for so many reasons that I feel as though I don't have a right to confront anybody about anything.
- I only confront when I'm really angry, and then it comes out all wrong and causes greater problems.
- I confront all the time, but I don't stop to think about how I do it, so it often backfires on me.

You will recognize that none of these descriptions qualify as constructive confrontation. If one or more of them fit you, it means that you need to improve your ability to confront.

The Fear of Confrontation

Fear is one of the major stumbling blocks to confrontation for most of us. Yet 2 Timothy 1:7 tells us, "For God did not give us a spirit of timidity, but a spirit of power, of love and of self-discipline."

"Timidity" is translated in other versions as "fear," but either way it's important to our discussion of confrontation. God doesn't want us to be fearful or timid when it comes to doing the right thing. If you are fearful or timid about confronting when you know you should, where is that spirit of timidity coming from? You can be sure it's not from God.

Ask yourself this question: Is there a person in your life at present that you know you need to confront about some situation or issue, but you have not yet done so? If your answer is yes, which of the following holds you back?

- I'm afraid of the other person's reaction.
- I don't know how to do it.
- I confronted that person once before, and it made things worse.
- I've confronted that person many times, and it doesn't do any good.
- I don't want to hurt her [his] feelings.
- I don't know if it is my place to confront that person or not.
- I've never been good at confrontation, and I'm fearful that I will make a fool out of myself.
- I'm waiting for the right time to do it (like maybe next century!).

Analyze your answer, and ask yourself if the root cause of your failure to confront is not indeed some kind of fear. Fear of rejection, fear of disapproval, fear of failure, fear of unpleasantness, etc. If fear is keeping you from confronting in a situation where you need to confront, then you are allowing that relationship to deteriorate instead of taking constructive steps to improve it.

Even though the other person may be at fault in his or her behavior or attitude, your refusal to confront is also a strong contributing factor in this troubled relationship. That means you need to take responsibility for the relationship, gird up your courage with prayer and planning, and confront so that there will be hope for the relationship to improve.

Constructive or Destructive?

Please note that this chapter is entitled "Confronting Constructively," which obviously infers that not all confrontation is constructive. And it is true that much confrontation ends up making matters worse because it was not done for the right motivation and in the right way.

Destructive Confrontation

Think of what is behind much confrontation that you observe. Many confrontations are motivated by anger, frustration, selfishness, "watching out for number one," or lack of patience—to name a few. The following examples illustrate common problems in the ways we approach confrontation.

Your boss calls the department together for a meeting, and, after some initial announcements and discussion, he or she announces that the quality of work has been extremely poor in a certain area. The boss then proceeds to ventilate a great deal of anger toward certain people, with warnings and threats of what will happen if the quality of their work does not improve. This is destructive confrontation because it is done in anger, in front of others, and in a humiliating and embarrassing manner.

A coworker calls you on the telephone and vents her anger because she just learned that you did not inform her about a meeting that took place yesterday. She felt she needed to be a part of that meeting and tells you in no uncertain terms how wrong you were not to include her. This is a destructive confrontation because it is done by phone instead of in person, and because it is done in haste and in anger. Some people use the telephone as their shield when they don't have the courage to confront in person.

Your boss calls you into his or her office and says, "You didn't reach your budget goals again this month. This is getting to be a troublesome pattern. There is no excuse for overspending in your travel budget, and I want you to bring it in line immediately." This is a destructive confrontation because the accusatory words will cause a defensive response and prevent any effective communication about the problem. The boss has assumed there is no good explanation even before giving you an opportunity to explain. Whether or not you have a sufficient excuse, this approach is likely to cause resentment, anger, and embarrassment on your part, and that will not motivate you or teach you how to solve the problem.

The Benchmarks of Constructive Confrontation

I want to emphasize that constructive confrontation, done for the benefit of the other person, may still be painful and unpleasant. Please don't equate comfort with constructive. There are few confrontations that are comfortable, and butterflies in your stomach are not proof that you should not confront.

But when you can honestly say that by confronting someone you can help that person to improve—provided he or she is willing to be helped—then that is a constructive motive and you should go forward with it.

There are some particular questions you can ask yourself in order to determine if a confrontation would be constructive or not.

If the confrontation were successfully completed, would the person you are confronting benefit from it? If so, then it would be a constructive confrontation. That doesn't mean that the confrontation would not be sensitive or cause some temporary pain. It doesn't mean that the person confronted would necessarily have a good first reaction to it. But, thinking beyond the immediate reaction, if that person were able to understand the need for the confrontation and that would cause some positive change, then it would be a benefit to him or her.

Does this situation or person really require confrontation, or do you need an attitude change or more patience? Sometimes we think the other person needs to be confronted in cases where we just need to be more patient and understanding. If you're confusing a need for patience with a need for confrontation, it's likely that a confrontation is not called for.

You know, people need time to grow and change, and some things just can't be speeded up; they take time. It's very important that we understand that sometimes we are called to endure patiently, even when there is a need to confront someone.

This is a lesson I have to continually relearn because I don't have a great deal of patience. God has to remind me that everyone doesn't have to march in my parade, at my speed, and that I can trust God to work on the other person at the right time, in the right way. God is not looking for a confrontation in every case of disagreement; sometimes he just wants *us* to learn a little more patience.

I remember a time when I decided to confront a woman at church because I didn't like her manner and attitude. I was right about her need to change, but my timing was wrong. She was a new believer, and she needed time to grow. My good friend advised me not to confront her. "Just role model what a godly woman is like," she said, "and she'll get the message."

Thankfully, I followed my friend's advice and waited. God has done a marvelous job at refining this woman, and she has grown immensely. She is teaching Bible studies now, and I've seen such a change in her attitude; she is much gentler and softer.

In his Letter to the Colossians Paul said, "Bear with each other and forgive whatever grievances you may have against one another" (Col 3:13). If we confront when God tells us to be patient and bear with a person, we can really make matters worse.

Is your desire to confront imbedded in a desire to get even or wrapped up in anger and vengeance? Any time our confrontation is tainted with wrong motives, it cannot be considered constructive, even if it is needed. That coworker may indeed need to be confronted, but if you do it simply because you're sick and tired of what that person is doing to you, then your motivation is totally selfish and suspect.

If you analyze the confrontations of Jesus, the times when he went head-on with other people—and there are many of those in the Gospels—you will notice that he was never confronting because of some personal agenda. He wasn't upset that his toes had been stepped on, rather that harm was being inflicted on others.

One of the red flags that warns me when a confrontation is not appropriate is when I'm thinking mostly about my rights being violated. You know what I mean. I'm thinking, "This is not fair to me." "I'm not going to put up with this." "How could they do this to me?" All of those are wrong motivations for confronting.

Speak the Truth in Love

"Speaking the truth in love" is a most important principle to apply when we are in confrontation mode. Any confrontation that we pursue has to be rooted in love for the other person if it is done correctly, with the right motivation. That "love" doesn't mean gushy feelings or even good feelings toward the person, but a God-type love that cares about the good of the other person. It is the Christ-love that is poured into our hearts by the Holy Spirit, the kind of love for others that you really can't know without the power of God's Spirit operating in your heart (see chapter four).

I remember when a new employee decided to confront me about something. It turned out to be a disaster for her and extremely uncomfortable for me. First, she chose the worst possible day to do so. She knew it was the worst possible day in a very busy week; she knew other urgent issues would distract me; yet she went ahead.

Second, she was very young, extremely inexperienced, and didn't know the facts at all. She had worked for us less than two months, so her knowledge level was totally inadequate.

She never stopped to think about whether she should confront, whether it was a good time, whether it was for the right reason, whether she had her facts straight, or whether she was interfering where she had no authority, right, or knowledge. In short, she looked at it through her own eyes, never considering the others involved, and barreled ahead.

I remember her saying to me, "But I prayed about it." Well, I don't doubt that she did. However, had she sought advice from any trusted counselor, they would have advised her against that confrontation, there's no doubt about it. Yet she had worked herself into an emotional state by allowing herself to imagine things that were not true and was convinced that because she prayed about it, it was the right thing to do.

Funny how all of us can convince ourselves we're doing the right thing because "we prayed about it." Praying about something incorrectly is not going to make it right. We can use prayer as a way to justify our behavior. So when you pray before a confrontation—and you should—ask God to reveal where your thinking may be wrong. Ask him to help you look at this from the other person's point of view, to look beyond the obvious or what appears to you, and ask yourself if you really know what's going on.

Many employees blame their bosses for things their bosses had nothing to do with. But because the employee doesn't know the whole story and isn't privy to all the information that the boss is, that employee may well initiate an inappropriate confrontation, assuming he or she is right without knowing the facts.

When you confront in those kinds of situations, do so with the understanding that you could be wrong. Don't set yourself up for embarrassment by accusations that turn out to be false simply because you didn't have the whole story.

Tips for Confronting

Once you've come to the conclusion that you truly need to confront a person about some situation, you need to consider several important elements of a confrontation. Remember that confronting is by nature sensitive and delicate and therefore needs to be thoughtfully approached. A reckless, speedy, unplanned confrontation can lead to disaster. Here are two proverbs that give us some good advice on confronting:

> A simple man believes anything, but a prudent man gives thought to his steps.
>
> PROVERBS 14:15

> A patient man has great understanding, but a quick-tempered man displays folly.
>
> PROVERBS 14:29

A prudent person would be the opposite of a quick-tempered person. The admonition of these passages is that we should approach any type of a confrontation with careful thought, prudently, not rashly, and carefully, not in the heat of emotion.

Choose the right time. The timing of your confrontation is critical. Which of these situations would be appropriate for a confrontation?

- You are upset and at the point of tears.
- You spent a sleepless night worrying about it.
- The "confrontee" is extremely busy this week.

- The "confrontee" just had some bad news.
- You are angry.
- The "confrontee" has had a recent health problem.

Hopefully it is obvious that none of these would be good times for confrontation. Since it will be a delicate situation at best, try to choose a time that will help and not hinder the possibility of success. The timing has to be right for you and for the other person, as much as possible. "Sleep on it" is an old-fashioned but useful motto to keep in mind. Don't confront in haste. Let your anger subside. Give yourself time to prepare so that you are in control and you can make certain your motives are correct.

Then choose a time suitable for the other person. For example, don't choose a very busy workday, the last minute before quitting, or a time when the other person is obviously exhausted or preoccupied with some other matter.

It should also be noted, however, that some confrontations can't wait. The following situations are examples.

- It is now or never. There will be no further opportunity.
- The situation is so volatile and full of potential harm that to wait could endanger the reputation or welfare of others.
- The name of Jesus Christ would be dishonored by waiting.
- Your ethics or morality could be misunderstood or defamed by waiting.

Choose the right place. Not only is the right time important, but the right place is as well. Here are the basic things to remember in choosing the right place:

- Choose a private place where you can have a one-on-one discussion without being overheard by others. You may want to consider the implications of calling someone into your office and shutting the door. That could be a signal to others that a confrontation is occurring, so even though it is in a private place, it may still need to be more discreet.
- Consider an off-site location. That is a good idea, especially in what you would consider "high profile" situations.
- Consider confronting over a meal. It seems to break down some barriers when we share a meal with someone.

Avoid finger-pointing. Finger-pointing phrases and words are those that put people on the defensive.

- "You never are on time ..."
- "You've made the same mistake three times ..."
- "You don't know how to do this ..."
- "You have difficulty getting along with others in the department ..."
- "Your attitude is causing problems ..."
- "You never listen to me ..."
- "You have had your way for too long ..."

Notice that all these statements begin with "you." Now think how you react to finger-pointing when it comes your way. It causes you to be defensive, it hurts your feelings, and it can cause you to retreat, to argue, to get angry—and more. It often generates a combination of those reactions.

Remember, we are aiming at constructive confrontation, an outcome that will be beneficial to everyone—a win-win solution—so we need to choose words carefully. Alternatives that could avoid putting the other person on the defensive include:

- "Perhaps there has been a misunderstanding ..."
- "I could be wrong, but ..."
- "I'm sure it was not intentional on your part, but ..."
- "If my information is correct,..."
- "It is my understanding ..."
- "You may not be aware, but ..."
- "I know you meant no harm, but ..."

Plan your words. Proverbs 21:23 reminds us that "he who guards his mouth and his tongue keeps himself from calamity." Guarding your words carefully is always important, but never more so than when you are confronting someone. How you say what you have to say will make a big difference in whether the confrontation is a success or a failure.

This advice from Proverbs 16:21 is very relevant: "The wise in heart are called discerning, and pleasant words promote instruction." The purpose of a constructive confrontation is instructive—right? We want to positively instruct someone else so that he or she is motivated to change. Well, pleasant words promote instruction, or as another translation puts it, "Sweetness of speech increases persuasiveness" (NAB).

That doesn't mean that we have to be gushy, and we certainly don't want to be phony. It just means we are wise enough to choose words that can be swallowed as easily as possible.

I remember when I had to confront a new employee, realizing that I had made a mistake in hiring her for the position. It was a major mismatch, and I should have seen it in advance. But having made a hasty decision, I was now faced with correcting it.

Knowing how fragile her self-image was, I decided to ease the blow by assuming all responsibility. I told her that it was my mistake and allowed her to make the decision of whether to stay or not. (I was fairly certain she would not stay, which made it easier to give her the option.)

She ventilated a good bit on me, and I saw no need to defend or explain. She would be leaving to go somewhere else, and she didn't need to have her confidence shaken any more than it was already. Besides, it didn't hurt me to listen to what she believed to be true, even though I knew it wasn't.

Had I thought I could have helped her by confronting her with detailed explanations and examples of why her work was most unsatisfactory, perhaps I would have done so. But my sense was that she just wasn't strong enough to face it and it could have been a terrible blow to her. I didn't want that to happen, so I chose to be the "fall guy." Sometimes that may be the wise course that God shows you to use.

Occasions for Constructive Confrontation

There are certain situations that are common in the work-place and do call for constructive confrontation. Let's look at some of them.

Careless Mistakes

These are mistakes that arise simply from a lack of attention to details, but they are affecting your ability to do your job, as well compromising the quality of work produced by your division or company. Even though you are simply this person's co-worker, not his or her manager, this qualifies as a situation that needs some constructive confrontation. In most cases, it is best to try to confront this individual directly before taking it to a higher level.

So you decide to summon your courage and talk with this coworker. You choose a day when the workload is manageable, and you invite her to have lunch with you in a secluded set-ting, where your conversation can be kept private. You need to approach the topic in a way that doesn't sound like finger-pointing, yet you have to get to the point and be specific in order to accomplish anything positive.

Which approach would work best? You could say, "As you know, I've been working here for almost twelve years, and since you're somewhat new on the job, I thought it would be good to give you a few pointers because you are making some mistakes that are causing a lot of problems. Let me point out to you what you are doing wrong ..."

Or you could try saying something like, "I remember when I first started working here, everything was so new and confusing. I'm sure I made tons of mistakes, but there was a woman who really helped me, and so I thought maybe I could do the same for you. There are some areas where a few changes could make things easier for you and help us get the work processed better, with fewer customer complaints. For example ..."

The first approach has a finger-pointing feel to it, doesn't it? The clues to that include lines like, "...since you're somewhat new on the job," "...you are making some mistakes," and, "...let me point out to you what you are doing wrong..." This approach will generate an immediate defensive reaction, communication will probably shut down after the first paragraph, and it will most likely result in making matters worse.

A few word changes can make a world of difference in the results. Notice the more constructive words and phrases in the second approach: "I thought maybe I could do the same for you," and, "a few changes could make things easier for you."

Also notice the "let-them-off-the-hook" opening. You give the person you are confronting an excuse, if you will, so that they don't need to be so defensive. It's always helpful to be vulnerable about yourself and share anything that will indicate you aren't perfect either.

Confronting Poor Work Habits
Poor work habits that often need confronting include frequently being late, not meeting deadlines, doing sloppy work, and failing to follow policies or guidelines.

Let's say that you are a manager or supervisor and one of your employees is habitually late to work. Choosing a good time, you call this employee into your office to discuss some other business-related issue so as not to put that person on the defensive. Then at the conclusion of that discussion you broach the touchy subject of being on time. How could you best approach the subject?

First, you could say, "Before you go, let me point out something that is bothering me. You've been late to work a lot, and it just drives me crazy. I want every person here on time every day. You're paid to be here on time, so I'll be expecting you to be on time every day from now on. I hope that is clear."

Or you could say, "I've noticed that you have some difficulty getting to work on time. Is there a problem? If there's a good reason, perhaps you need to tell me so we can work it out, say, by cutting your lunchtime or having you work later each day."

Notice that the focus of the first approach is the manager: "It just drives me crazy," "I want every person here on time," "I'll be expecting you to be on time." Again, this is not likely to generate a desire to comply.

It is far better to motivate people to want to do what is right, if possible, rather than use authority to demand it. The second approach would be most likely to generate a good result because it should not put the other person on the defensive. It gives them a hook, if you please, and doesn't accuse without asking for an explanation.

An Attitude Problem

Perhaps one of the most difficult confrontations is one about attitude. If someone has a negative, wrong attitude, it makes a confrontation less likely to succeed. Yet a bad attitude does more harm than almost anything else you can name.

Let's say you work with a person who is always negative,

griping, complaining, and unhappy about everything. Consider these two confrontation approaches.

The first goes something like, "I've noticed that your attitude is always negative. You never seem to be happy about anything, and that makes it difficult to work with you. Your attitude really poisons the atmosphere, so I wanted to suggest that you work at being more positive."

On the other hand, a more constructive approach might go, "I've noticed that you are often unhappy about the job and the people here. I'm not trying to pry, but I was just wondering if there is any way that I can help you. I'd be glad to try, because I'm sure you realize that attitudes tend to be contagious. When one person gets down, it tends to pull others down as well. Maybe there are some positive steps we could take to help you change your attitude." Notice that this approach avoids the finger-pointing and leaves some room for discussion.

To Confront or Not to Confront

If you are not a manager but know of some poor work habits of coworkers that need to be confronted (and management either doesn't see or refuses to confront), what course of action should you take? Talk to the manager and try to encourage him or her to confront? Talk to the coworker and try to settle it between the two of you? Do nothing if it doesn't affect you directly? Do nothing even if it does affect you directly?

This "to confront or not to confront" decision is not a black-and-white one. Each situation calls for careful consideration on your part, coupled with much prayer for guidance and wisdom. If you are not a person's direct manager, before you decide to confront, ask yourself these questions:

- Is it highly likely that this person will see this as inappropriate on my part? Will it be seen as "sticking my nose in someone else's business"?
- Is my relationship with this person of such a nature that he or she is likely to be open to my suggestions or confrontation and perhaps even appreciative that I came to him or her directly?
- Does this person's poor work habit have a direct negative impact on our company, profit, customers, or productivity?
- Does this person's poor work habit have a direct negative impact on my ability to do my job well?
- Am I just irritated that this person is getting by with poor work habits when I do it right?

The answers to these questions will give you some insight into whether you are the appropriate person to confront or not.

When Confrontation Backfires

I've encouraged you not to avoid confrontation when it is the right thing to do. But we also have to be aware that even constructive confrontation doesn't always work. Solomon warned us that people will not always listen or change when confronted.

Whoever loves discipline loves knowledge, but he who hates correction is stupid.

PROVERBS 12:1

He who heeds discipline shows the way to life, but whoever ignores correction leads others astray.

PROVERBS 10:17

The way of a fool seems right to him, but a wise man listens to advice.

PROVERBS 12:15

There are no guarantees about how a constructive confrontation will turn out, no matter how pure your motives or how well you choose your words. It may turn out well, even opening up fruitful new avenues of communication. On the other hand, the person may be totally quiet, showing no response at all. Or he or she may become angry and irrational, defensive, or act very hurt and emotional. Perhaps the person will simply refuse to change. It may well be that he or she will be too defensive, or too insecure or too arrogant, even to hear what you say. Just remember, you have control over what you do in the situation but not over the other person's inward characteristics, experience, or state of mind.

It is possible there will be a delayed positive response. It often happens that at the moment of confrontation a person reacts in an out-of-control manner, but after some thought and introspection, he or she is able to hear your concerns and come back with the right response.

Personal Performance Review

Unless confrontation comes easy for you (and if it does, you probably have not read this far in this chapter!), I would strongly urge you to make a plan for any confrontation that is needed.

I know it will help you greatly and you will begin to improve this skill. This is especially important for those of you in management positions.

The next time you find a confrontation necessary, first sit down with paper and pencil and write out a plan. The following simple format for such a plan will make certain you've done your preliminary homework and give you the confidence you need to move ahead.

My Plan for Confrontation

I need to confront [name] in order to help [her/him].
   Before I confront, I will
   - pray for wisdom and guidance.
   - seek needed advice, if appropriate.
   - examine my motives to make certain I am doing it for the right reason.
   - make certain I am not acting out of anger or vengeance.

The best time for this confrontation is _____
The best place for this confrontation is _____
I will open the conversation by saying_____

Regardless of the immediate results or reaction, I will trust God to work this out to his glory.

Chapter 8

Biblical Principle #8

Go the Extra Mile

She had lost her husband early in her marriage. Her brother-in-law also died, leaving another young widow named Orpah. Her mother-in-law, Naomi, also a widow, was leaving to go back to her homeland, for she was living in a foreign land when her husband and sons died.

Naomi said to her two daughters-in-law, "Go back, each of you, to your mother's home. May the Lord show kindness to you, as you have shown to your dead and to me. May the Lord grant that each of you will find rest in the home of another husband" (Ru 1:8b-9a). No one would have questioned that these young women should return to their own homes, where they would have hope of a future. There was no good reason not to, and Orpah decided to do just that.

But Ruth replied, "Don't urge me to leave you or to turn back from you. Where you go I will go, and where you stay I will stay. Your people will be my people and your God my God" (Ru 1:16).

Ruth did far more than was requested or required of her. She was willing to go the extra mile. And at first it surely appeared to be a poor choice. She and Naomi lived in poverty, and she had to glean the fields to gather leftover grain for their food. This was demeaning and dangerous work, but Ruth humbled herself and kept going the extra mile.

You know the end to this beautiful story. As she worked in his field, Boaz noticed her and her dedication to Naomi. Before long wedding bells were ringing, and Ruth married Boaz. One of their children, Obed, became the grandfather of King David. Had Ruth not been willing to go the extra mile, she would have missed this incredible blessing.

We too are called to be extra-milers. Jesus was pretty clear about this.

> You have heard that it was said, "Eye for eye, and tooth for tooth." But I tell you, do not resist an evil person. If someone strikes you on the right cheek, turn to him the other also. And if someone wants to sue you and take your tunic, let him have your cloak as well. If someone forces you to go one mile, go with him two miles.
>
> MATTHEW 5:38-41

This is absolutely revolutionary teaching, and I have to tell you that I still find it hard to swallow at times. It is in exact opposition to our culture. We are obsessed with our individual rights, and we are ready to fight anyone who would even think of infringing on them. And here Christ teaches us to let people take from us what they don't deserve and not retaliate. Again, this has to be a God-thing in our lives because human nature would never respond in this unselfish way. But that is what Jesus would do, and we are called to follow in his steps.

What does it mean to have an extra-mile attitude, to turn

the other cheek or to give your cloak as well as your shirt? What is Jesus trying to teach us? Does this mean as Christians in the workplace we are expected to:

- endure unfair treatment without griping or complaining?
- endure any kind of treatment?
- put up with unacceptable behavior or habits from others forever?
- never say anything negative to anyone?

No, an extra-mile attitude is not a recipe for abuse. It is not the road to becoming a doormat. There is a balance to find in this extra-mile principle. I believe that while Jesus is exhorting us to do more than we have to do, he is also setting boundaries on how far we go and how much we do.

For sure, an extra-mile attitude will cause us to:

- refrain from saying some of the things we would like to say
- do some work we don't have to do or want to do
- put in extra time and effort to help a person
- endure some unkind words or treatment
- have patience and tolerance with others who are not as experienced or knowledgeable as we are

Let me relate a real experience that one woman shared with me. She worked in an office with several other women, most of them younger than she was. This woman had a very strong work ethic, but the younger women didn't seem to share it. As a result she did much more than her share of the work.

As she talked to me, I could hear the bitterness and resentment that had built up over the many months. She said, "I really can't be nice to them anymore. They make me so angry with their lazy attitude, as though the company owed them something for nothing. In fact, it's gotten to the place where I just avoid them as much as possible; some days we don't even speak to each other."

I think we can all relate to her feelings and reactions. The irony of this predicament was that although she was doing more than was required of her, actually going the extra mile, her good deeds were not opening an avenue of love with her coworkers. Indeed, her actions contributed to the conflict because she resented what she did for them and they knew it.

As I was talking with this woman, my first instinct was to say to her, "Listen, you shouldn't put up with this. You've put up with too much already. Go back there and talk to management. Get this thing out in the open. Fight!"

But we have to keep remembering that as Christians our manager is God. We are first of all accountable to him, even before we are accountable to our company or management. Going the extra mile may not have been this woman's duty to the company, but indeed it may have been her duty to God. The problem was that she had allowed her resentful attitude to build so much that the extra-mile effort became a hindrance rather than an asset to her testimony as a Christian.

I'm sure that some of you have done something similar. There are many of us who overstep the boundaries and end up in resentfulness. Whose fault is that? It's our own, really. We've allowed ourselves to become victims, and that is not what Jesus meant by "extra-miling" it.

However, for every person who goes too many extra miles, there are numbers of others who refuse to go the first one, don't you think? So pray for proper balance, but please, don't let the culture around you rob you of practicing this Christ-like attitude.

Our Call to Be Self-Motivated
How hard do you work when no one is looking? It's a good measure of your extra-mile attitude. Here's what Proverbs 6:6-8 says about self-motivation:

Go to the ant, you sluggard: consider its ways and be wise!
It has no commander, no overseer or ruler, yet it stores its
provision in summer and gathers its food at harvest.

Ants are self-motivated creatures. Without anyone standing over them and telling them what to do, they perform their jobs diligently and are prepared for what lies ahead.

A Christian in the workplace should be like the ant: self-motivated and willing to dig in and get the work done without prompting, without constant supervision. Does your manager trust you? Can she or he be assured that you will diligently do your job whether anyone is watching or not? Certainly a Christian should produce that kind of reputation.

Our witness in the world can never be effective if our lives aren't different. If we have the "It's not my job" attitude that is prevalent today, if we drag our feet and do only what we're told to do, or if we gripe and complain about doing anything above and beyond our job description, how will our coworkers and management know that Christ makes a difference in our lives? They won't, and our verbal witness, if there is one, will fall on deaf ears.

As Christians we have a power far beyond self to help motivate us: we have God's Holy Spirit dwelling within us to give us the strength we need. We should have an outstanding testimony on our jobs through doing our work, doing it whether anyone's watching or not, doing it to the best of our ability, and being willing to go the extra mile.

Personal Performance Review

Which of the following things have you done on your job in the last six months that were *not* required of you?

- stayed late to finish a project on time
- taught a coworker a skill he or she needed to know
- helped solve a coworker's equipment problem
- suggested and did an additional project or job that would improve company operation, product, or service
- did a job over to improve the quality or result
- cleaned the kitchen or coffee machine, etc., when it wasn't your turn
- made coffee when it wasn't your turn
- covered the phones for someone else
- did something for your boss to relieve some of his or her workload
- loaned some equipment or other resources to a coworker
- offered to help a coworker who was in a bind

What could you add to this list?

How would you evaluate your extra-mile attitude?

- I go extra miles on a regular basis.
- I go extra miles occasionally.
- I resist doing anything not required of me.
- I go too many extra miles.

If you resist going extra miles, or do so rarely, can you determine why you are not an "extra-miler"? Which reason fits best?

- I have so much work to do that there is no time for picking up someone else's slack.
- No one ever offers to help me, and therefore I don't offer to help others.
- I resent having to go extra miles when it is never appreciated.
- I have a lazy streak and tend to have a "just get by" attitude.
- If I go an extra mile one time, it will be expected of me all the time.

Can you think of an extra mile-activity that you could do in the next week? Are you willing to do it?

Chapter 9

Biblical Principle #9
Mend Broken Relationships

He was the rebellious child, the strong-willed son, the one who had to try his wings. So he took his part of his father's money and went out on his own. In a short time he had squandered all his money, had soiled the family name with his reckless living, and was absolutely destitute.

He finally came to his senses and recognized his true condition, then decided to go back to his father and beg for a position as a servant. That would be much better than his current situation.

You know this beautiful parable of the Prodigal Son, found in the fifteenth chapter of Luke. As the son returned to his home, his father saw him from afar and ran to welcome him. The father forgave his errant son, restored his position in the family, and threw a party to celebrate.

This picture of forgiveness almost boggles our minds. I would have jerked the young man by his collar and lectured him about his total failure. I would have made him earn his right to come back to the family fold. I would have told him he had to suffer the consequences of his actions. I would have reminded him that his older brother was the good boy and reprimanded him for not being more like his brother.

But as Jesus told this parable, the father did none of those things. Just the opposite. He rushed out to forgive. He couldn't forgive fast enough. The son's past was put behind him and he had a clean slate because the father was into forgiveness and restoration, not retribution or vengeance.

Jesus told us this parable to teach us about our heavenly Father's willingness to forgive and restore us. And he taught us how we should forgive others and give people a second chance; how we should do everything we can to restore a broken relationship.

If relationships are the sandpaper of our lives, broken relationships are surely the steamrollers of life. They flatten us like pancakes and often leave us feeling empty, rejected, deeply hurt, and emotionally damaged.

A woman told me that she couldn't take part as usual in her family's Christmas celebration because her brother would be there and she is not speaking to her brother any longer. She began to explain the reason their relationship is broken, and it seemed from her side of the story that she had a reason to feel hurt. But the break in that relationship was not only very painful to her, it caused problems for her sons as well when they were not able to take part in an important family occasion.

The thirty-year marriage of a friend of mine is now broken. It's not her fault, and she is doing all she can to repair it, but her pain has been palpable.

Another friend was "downsized" from an organization, and she felt the decision was extremely unfair. It came from people she had trusted as more than just her employer and manager; she had seen them as friends. Now that work relationship is severed, it has caused an ongoing rift between her and the managers she once respected.

Think of the broken relationships in your own world, whether they are yours personally or those you are aware of. Consider the ripple effect that broken and hurting relationships have, touching not only the people directly involved but inevitably many others as well.

Are we doomed to have to live with these broken relationships? What is our duty and responsibility in trying to mend a broken relationship? That is what we will consider in this chapter.

Jesus' "Fix" for Broken Relationships

Chapters five to seven of Matthew contain what we call the Sermon on the Mount, the mountainside discourse Jesus delivered by the Sea of Galilee to his disciples and other followers. Most of it deals with relationships of one type or another and gives us very clear guidelines on how to improve our relationships.

Consider what Jesus taught us to do when a relationship has been broken or wounded.

Therefore, if you are offering your gift at the altar and there remember that your brother has something against you, leave your gift there in front of the altar. First go and be reconciled to your brother; then come and offer your gift.

MATTHEW 5:23-24

Offering Your Gift at the Altar

The people on that mountainside would have readily understood this illustration. Anyone offering a gift at the altar would be a religious person, one who took his or her commitment seriously. In using this setting, I believe Jesus is trying to teach us

- that even committed people who are trying to do the right thing will have relationship struggles
- that mending broken relationships takes priority over religious activities and duties
- that you can't substitute spiritual activity for trying to mend a broken relationship

Remember That Your Brother Has Something Against You

Here "brother" refers to those who are in relationship with us because we share a common humanity. The term is not limited to blood relationships or Christian brotherhood.

Jesus says, "... And there *remember* that your brother has something against you." That would seem to imply that it is possible to *forget* that you have a broken relationship. Since broken relationships are painful, denial can be one way people deal with them. That denial can take several forms:

- staying very busy, even if it means creating unnecessary activity
- convincing oneself that there's nothing that can be done about it
- convincing oneself that the one who caused the problem should initiate the reconciliation

- finding other relationships to fill the gaps in life left by the broken one
- nursing hurt feelings and letting pride and stubbornness prevent action

If you were ever guilty of conveniently "forgetting" that you needed to try to heal a broken relationship, which of these reasons applied to you?

- didn't know what to say or how to say it
- were fearful of being rejected
- were afraid you'd make matters worse
- found it difficult to say, "I'm sorry"
- thought it was more the other person's fault than yours, and therefore the first move was up to him or her
- just couldn't find the right time to do it
- were just too proud or stubborn to do anything about it
- always have difficulty facing issues head-on and tend to run away from problems

As I've already noted, the first step to improving our relationships is to admit to our own mistakes. If you are willing to let God's Spirit probe into your heart, you may discover that you are harboring a wrong attitude that needs to be cleaned out. While it may be true that most of the problem is with the other person, rarely is it true that all the blame can be laid at one person's feet.

Pray David's prayer: "Search me, O God, and know my heart; test me and know my anxious thoughts. See if there is any offensive way in me, and lead me in the way everlasting"

(Ps 139:23-24). Once you admit your role in the broken relationship, minor as it may be, and confess that to the Lord and make yourself willing to do whatever you can to mend this relationship, you are going to feel as if the Empire State Building has just been taken off your shoulders.

The phrase "has something against you" is also worth a second look. Could it be that, while most of us are very good at remembering what others have done wrong, we too easily forget our own wrongs in relationships? It's possible the problem is even one that doesn't strike us as especially memorable—hurt feelings, misunderstandings, hastily spoken or ill-chosen words, or simply neglect.

What another has against us may actually be a product of his or her own imagination, or simply a misconception. Whatever the case, though, if it has caused a rift in the relationship, it needs to be addressed.

You may sometimes find that this principle of dealing with broken relationships needs to be applied the other way around too. In fact, even if you are the injured party, God may direct you to take the first step.

I met a young woman who told me of her struggle with her relationship with her father. He had never been a good father to her, and now she longed to have him apologize for the pain he had caused her. Repeatedly she prayed that God would cause her father to be willing to apologize.

But as she studied the Bible, God clearly told her that she needed to ask for her father's forgiveness. Though she had far less to apologize for than he did, she saw the part she had played and realized she wasn't totally innocent. So, in obedience, she asked her father to forgive her.

He was dumbfounded. He knew as well as she did that her offenses were very minor compared to his. He wasn't able to return the apology, and he may never do that, but this young woman knew she had done what God wanted her to do, and it truly set her free from the emotional baggage she had been carrying for so long.

Leave Your Gift at the Altar

Why would it be necessary to "leave your gift there in front of the altar" in order to be reconciled? Jesus is illustrating the urgency and importance of addressing these broken relationships. He says, in effect, as soon as you are aware that someone has something against you, reconciliation should become your highest priority.

Think of the culture in which this was written. If someone were at the altar performing the sacred duty of offering a sacrifice as prescribed by Jewish law, it would be a very drastic action to leave that gift in front of the altar without completing the ritual. Jesus knew that using this image would clearly convey the importance he placed on reconciliation.

Think of relationship problems over your years at work, in your church, and in your family. Which of the following have you witnessed because of failures to be reconciled, your own or someone else's?

- The break in the relationship grew deeper and wider.
- The reason for the break was exaggerated and amplified way beyond reality.
- Innocent people were hurt because the relationship was not reconciled.

- Gossip and backbiting increased.
- The longer the problem was neglected, the more difficult it was to resolve.
- It opened the door for illegitimate or harmful relationships to begin.
- It caused a church split.
- It caused a family split.
- It caused other relationships to deteriorate.
- It caused great financial stress.
- It adversely affected someone's testimony for Jesus Christ.
- It caused nonbelievers to have negative impressions of true believers.
- It caused those involved to walk away from their commitment to Jesus Christ, or otherwise had a seriously detrimental effect on them spiritually.

That's a long list and it's not exhaustive. The longer we put off needed reconciliation, the more these consequences and others will be realized, as I'm sure you have observed.

Make the First Move

Jesus said, "First go...." That's a directive, right? Not a suggestion, but a direct command. And who is to go? We are. Jesus teaches that we should make the first move even if we're not the one at fault, and do it quickly.

This goes against the advice you will receive from most "earthly advisors." They are more likely to give you some of the following advice:

- It's his [her] problem, not yours. Let the other person make the first move.
- Don't let that person manipulate you with hurt feelings.
- Some relationships are doomed; let it go.
- He [she] needs to grow up and learn a few lessons.

The world's approach is always focused on the self, but letting go of what your human nature wants to do and being willing to do it God's way is what Jesus meant by losing your life in order to gain it.

Notice that Jesus put no qualifiers in his directive. He said, if there is a rift in your relationship with another person, go quickly and try to repair it, regardless of the circumstances. To do so is, of course, humbling, and will no doubt be uncomfortable, but we need to act on what we know is right, not be controlled by our feelings.

One of the things I've been learning about my relationship with the Lord is that my initial reaction is almost always a human, self-centered one. I had thought that someday I would outgrow that, and maybe I will, but it hasn't happened yet. What I do see, however, is that as I grow in grace and become a more mature Christian, I am more and more able to ignore that first, sinful reaction and do what God wants me to do. It is a matter of acting our way into the right feelings, rather than waiting for the right feelings to motivate us into action.

Go and Be Reconciled

The dictionary definition of reconciliation is to cause to cease hostility or opposition; to restore and make good again; to repair. Therefore if you are going to attempt reconciliation with someone who has something against you, you would likely *not* do the following:

- repeat all the mistakes he or she has made and where he or she is wrong
- defend yourself and explain why you are not at fault
- tell how you have been hurt
- lecture the other person about his or her need to change

Oh, it will be tempting to recite your side of the story, but if reconciliation is your goal, let go of your right to have your pound of flesh, to prove you are right, or to get in your two cents' worth. More appropriately you could

- lovingly accept blame for whatever you have done that has contributed to the bad feelings
- talk about what you are willing to do to mend the relationship
- explain how important the relationship is to you
- establish some guidelines that hopefully will help avoid similar misunderstandings or hurts in the future

Don't confuse reconciliation with confrontation. Reconciliation is to cease hostility. Confrontation is for the purpose of stating grievances and changing behavior. Sometimes it is necessary to confront before reconciliation is possible, but not always.

In 1 Samuel 15 the Lord rejected Saul as king because of Saul's disobedience. When the prophet Samuel asked Saul, "Why did you not obey the Lord?" he responded, "But I did obey the Lord." Like us he tried hard to justify his actions, for he did obey—but only partially. Samuel replied to Saul, "Does the Lord delight in burnt offerings and sacrifices as much as in obeying the voice of the Lord? To obey is better than sacrifice" (1 Sm 15:22).

What Jesus said in the Sermon on the Mount was really what Samuel had said to King Saul. Yes, God wants us to do the religious activities we do, but he is looking for obedience more than anything else, and he wants us to make patching up broken relationships our highest priority.

Is It Always Possible to Be Reconciled?

The first verse we considered in the introduction gives us some insight into the answer to this question: "If it is possible, as far as it depends on you, live at peace with everyone" (Rom 12:18). If you have a broken relationship, make certain that you have done and are doing everything you can to mend that relationship. Don't let yourself off the hook easily. Go the extra mile, humble yourself, initiate the reconciliation, be willing to swallow your pride ... whatever you can do to effect true reconciliation.

However, please keep in mind that being reconciled does not include

- being someone's "doormat"
- enduring abusive treatment of any kind
- compromising your Christian principles or integrity
- lowering your standards of behavior

It is not reconciliation at any price that we are seeking. It is true reconciliation, where from the heart the past can be put behind us, forgiveness can be given and received, and we can establish a new, better foundation for that relationship to go forward.

Dealing With the Aftermath of a Broken Relationship

It may be that we manage to be reconciled with someone without having had the relationship fully restored to its former state; too much damage may have been done earlier. Choices and actions produce consequences, and there is an aftermath that we must deal with. Words were spoken that cannot be unspoken. Feelings were aroused that cannot be quickly forgotten.

I want to encourage you to consider how Jesus dealt with his closest friends and associates, who failed him so miserably. As you know, Judas betrayed him, Peter denied him, Thomas doubted him, and they all fled when the soldiers came to arrest him. In fact, they all exhibited lack of faith and trust in him throughout his ministry. Yet see how Jesus dealt with Peter, for example, giving us a beautiful example of how to deal with a broken relationship:

When they had finished eating, Jesus said to Simon Peter, "Simon son of John, do you truly love me more than these?" "Yes, Lord," he said, "you know that I love you." Jesus said, "Feed my lambs."

Again Jesus said, "Simon son of John, do you truly love

me?" He answered, "Yes, Lord, you know that I love you."
Jesus said, "Take care of my sheep."

The third time he said to him, "Simon son of John, do you love me?"

Peter was hurt because Jesus asked him the third time, "Do you love me?" He said, "Lord, you know all things; you know that I love you." Jesus said, "Feed my sheep."

JOHN 21:15-17

Think of what has just taken place. Jesus was put on trial and crucified on a cross. Remember what happened in the Garden of Gethsemane, when all the disciples fled and left Jesus alone, and at the trial, where Peter denied even knowing Jesus. As far as we know, Peter was not even present at the crucifixion. There's no question that at this point their relationship had been wounded greatly. I imagine Peter was feeling very penitent and regretful and wondering if Jesus would ever allow him to be a close friend and disciple again.

Jesus could have legitimately said any of the following to Peter at this moment in time:

- "Peter, I can't begin to tell you how painful it was to hear you deny me three times in the midst of that mockery of a trial, with that crown of thorns on my head and the soldiers beating me."
- "Peter, at the Garden of Gethsemane, why did you run away when I needed you with me?"
- "Peter, I was so disappointed in you because you were the one who promised you would never leave me, even if you had to die with me."

- "Peter, I thought you loved me more than anyone else, but I guess you didn't because look how you left me and denied me."
- "Peter, you were supposed to be my rock, the one on whom I could always depend. Yet you were the first to deny me."
- "Peter, if you want to be my disciple, you're going to really have to change because I just can't depend on you anymore. Look how you deserted me."
- "Peter, if you want to be my disciple, you're going to have to prove yourself to me. It will take time, Peter. After the way you treated me, you can't expect to just waltz back in and take over, can you?"

Jesus had a right to say any of these things to Peter, but Jesus' purpose was reconciliation. He wanted to help Peter get past his terrible mistakes and move on to be the man Jesus knew he could be. So he didn't say any of these things to Peter. After all, Peter knew them anyway. And notice that Jesus made the first move to restore Peter, although Peter was the one who had broken the relationship by his denial of Jesus.

Jesus' one concern was to make sure Peter was prepared for the awesome challenge that was ahead of him, as he started that first church of believers and converted so many people to faith in Jesus Christ. Jesus did not allow his damaged feelings, his bruised ego, or a need for revenge to control his feelings or actions. Instead he kept his eye on the big picture, knew how important it was that his relationship with Peter be fully restored, and made sure that the reconciliation took place.

As I've studied how Jesus dealt with Peter, it has truly

touched my heart and shown me how often I don't follow his example. This is humility displayed in a remarkable way. Can you imagine how hurtful Peter's denial had been to Jesus? I'm sure he was crushed when Judas betrayed him, but after all, he wasn't as close to Judas as he was to Peter. And Peter was the one who declared his loyalty to Jesus over and over. Big-mouth Peter—*I'll never leave you; I'll never deny you; I'll die for you!* But he didn't come through. He wasn't the friend he claimed to be.

Jesus, being fully man, was as hurt as you and I would be if someone did that to us. Yet he didn't lash out at Peter, nor berate him, nor accuse him, nor punish him. What a demonstration of unconditional love.

Think about this: If Jesus had come back at Peter with a recital of all of his failings, and gone on and on about how disappointed he was in him, etc., etc., do you think that would have had as great an impact on Peter as the fact that Jesus didn't even mention it? I really believe that Peter was even more humbled because Jesus didn't say a word about it. After all, Peter was well aware of what he had done. And he was probably expecting Jesus to let him have it. He knew he deserved it. But instead Jesus just put the past behind him and went forward with Peter.

So remember in dealing with the aftermath of a broken relationship, do everything you can to let go of the pain and the bitterness and give the relationship a chance to blossom again.

Conclusion

I want to make sure that I've presented a balanced view in this chapter, and that no one thinks that every relationship must be reconciled at any cost. That is not possible, nor is it right.

Some of you have endured terrible abuse in relationships, and those relationships need to be severed, at least until there is absolute and long-term change in the other person. Others have relationships that have been so terribly damaged that, although some reconciliation has taken place, it is not possible to be fully restored.

But we still must be willing to go the extra mile when it comes to reconciling any relationship that has been broken if we possibly can. As much as it depends on us, let's follow the teaching and example of our Lord and seek to be reconciled.

Personal Performance Review

Is there a "broken relationship" between you and someone else on your job at present? If so, what steps, if any, have you taken to try to mend it?

If you have not taken any steps to mend a broken relationship, why not?

What positive action are you willing to take to make the first move toward reconciling a broken relationship?

Chapter 10

Biblical Principle #10

Work With Integrity and Without Compromise

A couple of men were preaching the gospel so powerfully that many people were being converted. This worried the religious leaders greatly, because they were threatened by the preachers' success, fearful that they would lose their followers.

As a result, these religious leaders issued an ultimatum to the itinerant preachers, commanding them not to speak or teach at all in the name of Jesus. "But Peter and John replied, 'Judge for yourselves whether it is right in God's sight to obey you rather than God. For we cannot help speaking about what we have seen and heard'" (Acts 4:19-20).

These newly transformed disciples of Jesus Christ were fearless in their passion to spread the gospel. Empowered by the Holy Spirit, they understood that their allegiance to Jesus took precedence over all other relationships, even to the religious legal authority of the day.

One of our challenges in relating to the people we work with and for is to determine where to draw the line between being excellent workers and respecting the authority of those in management, and our responsibility to the other relationships and commitments in our lives.

Jesus provided us with the guideline we need through his response to the Pharisees when they were trying to trap him. They had posed a question they figured would catch him off guard and cause him to indict himself with his own words.

> "Teacher, we know you are a man of integrity and that you teach the way of God in accordance with the truth. You aren't swayed by men, because you pay no attention to who they are. Tell us then, what is your opinion? Is it right to pay taxes to Caesar or not?"
>
> But Jesus, knowing their evil intent, said, "You hypocrites, why are you trying to trap me? Show me the coin used for paying the tax." They brought him a denarius, and he asked them, "Whose portrait is this? And whose inscription?" "Caesar's," they replied. Then he said to them, "Give to Caesar what is Caesar's and to God what is God's." When they heard this, they were amazed. So they left him and went away.
>
> MATTHEW 22:16-22

The Pharisees were trying to get Jesus to contradict himself. Jesus had been proclaiming that God does not regard one person higher than another and is not impressed with their hypocritical religiosity. If they could get him to say that Caesar was of no importance and they owed him no allegiance, then they would have Jesus in trouble with the law and could get him arrested.

But Jesus was too smart for their scheming, and in answering them he gave to all of us a very important biblical principle: "Give to Caesar what is Caesar's and to God what is God's."

Our allegiance to Jesus Christ does not relieve us of our duties to others, even to people who may not be godly. We are to be good citizens and employers, giving to others what is rightfully theirs.

What We Owe Our Employer

If we think of our employers as the Caesars in our lives, it will give us some very good guidance on our behavior and responsibilities as employees. Let's think about the things a Christian employee owes to the employer, the things that are rightfully the employer's, whether he or she is a Christian or not.

Hard Work

A Christian employee should always give his or her employer an honest day's work for the money received. If you have agreed to do a certain job for a certain paycheck, then you owe that work to your employer.

It's amazing to see how few people really work hard for their employers. If you've been in the working world very long, you've certainly seen many people who work maybe one hour in three. They spend much of their working day talking on the phone, taking care of personal matters, talking to a coworker, or just dragging their feet instead of working diligently.

As I was designing a training program for a client, one of my first tasks was to understand the problem and the people better. So I spent a good bit of time interviewing employees. I heard a constant complaint that they had too much work to do, the employer was asking too much of them. Finally I said to one employee, "Do you really think you're asked to do more than you can accomplish in eight hours of honest work?" She was very candid in answering me. She said, "Mary, we used to have to work four to five hours a day in an eight-hour shift. Now they want us to work seven."

It has become common for people to be offended if you ask them to give eight hours' work for eight hours' pay. The attitude seems to be that the employer owes us eight hours' pay for maybe four hours' work, and to ask more is really outrageous.

To give to our employers what is rightfully theirs, Christians should always give a full day's work and never take advantage of their employers by cheating them out of time and work that is due to them. Our work habits should be noticeably different from those who try to take advantage of the employer, and our attitude should be one of desiring to give the employer what is his or her rightful due—hard work for our pay.

Protection of Our Employer's Assets

What belongs to your employer is yours to use for business purposes, not for your own personal benefit. Those pencils and pads, paper clips, and file folders that are supplied by your employer should not end up in your desk at home, for your own use. Similarly, we need to watch telephone calls on our employer's tab, and our expense accounts should be meticulously honest and fair.

We need to realize that taking our employer's assets is simply stealing. I'm well aware that this is a common practice, and we don't think of it as stealing, but again, Christians have standards higher than those of this world's. And if we render to Caesar what is rightfully his, then we will be careful not to steal from our employers and to do everything we can to conserve their money and their assets.

Loyalty

As long as we're willing to take a paycheck from our employer, we owe him or her, or the company, respect and loyalty. It is a very common thing for employees to constantly talk negatively about their company or their boss. But a Christian should not be found stabbing his or her boss in the back or running down the company to others.

This should be a point of distinction for a Christian employee. It should be quite noticeable that you do not enter into the office gossip or character assassination of anyone—especially of your boss and employer. If you find you cannot give this respect and loyalty, then you should move on. It's wrong to work for someone and at the same time disparage or constantly gripe and complain about that employer.

What We Owe God on the Job

The other half of this principle is to give to God what is God's. Sometimes we can all too easily give to Caesar what belongs to God, and compromise our integrity in the process.

Honesty

God requires of us a life of integrity and honesty, and there is no such thing as a white lie. Lying for your employer is giving to Caesar what is due to God. An employer has no right to ask an employee to lie or deceive in any way.

You may be thinking, "But my boss tells me to lie for him. What do I do?" Well, if you can just avoid a confrontation by simply not lying, then I recommend that. For instance, instead of saying, "He's not in," when he is, say, "I'm sorry, he's not available." That's the truth, and you don't even have to make an issue of it.

However, if your boss explicitly asks you to lie for him or her, this is where you have to take a stand and not render to the boss what is not due to him or her. If the boss makes an issue out of it, you could simply say, "I'm awfully sorry, but I wouldn't lie for myself, and I'm just not willing to lie for you either. However, I think I could handle the situation acceptably in another way." Another thoughtful response might be, "If I would lie *for* you, how would you ever believe that I wouldn't lie *to* you?"

If your employer asks you to falsify reports or alter statistics to make them look better, know that this is another place where a Christian cannot render to Caesar what belongs to God. When obeying an employer would cause us to disobey a Christian principle, then our course of action is clear. We obey God rather than man. That may cost us a job; it may cost us promotions or favor with the bosses. There is a price for true discipleship. But there should be no question as to what is right for us to do.

Honorable Activity
Socializing after work or with customers is the American way, but frequently it is not the godly way. There are jobs where dishonorable after-hours activity is common and expected, and the people who get ahead are those who take part. If

you're expected to participate in social occasions where lewd conversation or behavior is common, then you have a decision to make: Will you render to Caesar what belongs to God?

No employer has a right to require you to be a part of compromising situations in order to keep your job. That is not the employer's rightful due.

Appropriate Balance in Our Use of Energy and Time

If we must constantly give our employer twelve hours a day and weekends, we're probably giving to Caesar what belongs to God. While it's true we owe an honest day's work, if we give far more than that in order to get ahead or to please the boss, so that there's no time left for our families, our friends, our church, or ourselves, then we're getting into spiritually dangerous territory.

This one is tough to deal with because we feel guilty if others are working long hours and we are not. Or we worry about what others will think about us for not being there on Sunday to work. Again, it may be a costly decision, for it's true that some employers expect every drop of your time and energy in return for your job or in order for you to get promotions. But don't be fooled by this world's false standards of excellence. We owe God time and a balanced lifestyle, and if you put him first, he'll honor that commitment.

A young woman with a high executive position recently called to ask my advice in dealing with a difficult situation on her job. As she told me of the conflict and the manipulative, political environment in which she found herself, she said, "You know, this job so exhausts me and consumes me that I don't have time for things I really want to do." She went on to say that she used to be involved in caring ministries, but now there was no time or energy for that.

As soon as she told me that, the red flags went up. I asked her if she was not giving to Caesar what belonged to God. The warning signs were evident. The job was consuming her, causing great conflict within her, and robbing her of time and energy for ministry work.

Sometimes, especially when we are in a job that is prestigious and pays well, we are reluctant to realize that the job is not indispensable to our lives. I reminded this young woman that "it's just a job." In other words, you can walk away from it and still have your life. You don't have to have that job.

I think that was a new thought for her. She had worked hard to get where she was, and she was understandably proud of her achievement, but now the job she had wanted so badly was a great burden and causing multiple problems in her life. It was time for her to evaluate whether she was giving to her job what she should have been giving to God.

Remember that someday we will all stand before God and give an account for everything we've done. Do you ever think about that? What will you say if you've failed to give to your company what is rightfully theirs? What will you say if you have given your boss or career what really belongs to God and have compromised your standards and principles? When we get an eternal viewpoint and see things the way God sees them, it sure makes a difference.

Relationship Priorities

This "Caesar principle" also gives us guidelines in the relationship priorities of our lives. All of us have a variety of relationships in our lives, with differing demands on our time and commitment. If we are confused about where our loyalties lie, we can make disastrous decisions and cause great harm to these relationships. If we don't understand what God requires of us when it comes to relationship commitments, we can easily be fooled by what our culture tells us and base our relationship decisions on lies rather than God's truth.

We can generally divide the relationships of our lives into two broad categories that I like to call covenant relationships and contractual relationships. This will help us to see our relationships from God's perspective, and therefore make wiser decisions concerning them.

Covenant Relationships

This is a coined term, not a biblical one, but it is based on biblical principles. The Bible tells us of many covenants, and we learn that God takes covenants very seriously. The first covenant we read about in Scripture is God's covenant with Noah.

Genesis 9 goes into the details of that covenant, and you will notice that it contains both specific promises that God makes to Noah and his descendants and specific requirements God placed on them. Those are the conditions of the covenant.

Genesis 15 describes the covenant God made with Abram (later called Abraham), an unconditional covenant giving Abram's descendants the Promised Land. In 2 Samuel 7 God makes a covenant with David (the Davidic covenant), which promises that his throne will last forever. And there are other Old Testament examples of covenants between God and his people.

The good news of the New Testament is that Jesus Christ came to bring us a new covenant with God. Hebrews 7:22 says that "Jesus has become the guarantee of a better covenant"; this covenant is superior to the old one and promises us eternal life with God. So all of us who are born from above are now under the new covenant that was provided for us through the death and resurrection of Jesus Christ.

So we see that a covenant is an understood agreement between two or more people to do or not to do something specified in the covenant. God made covenants and considered them very serious matters.

Rarely if ever do we have formal documents defining the responsibilities of our relationships. Prenuptial agreements have become common these days, but they are simply for the protection of the individuals and their property. They do not establish relationship responsibilities and commitments, so they would not qualify as covenants.

However, based on what we know about God's priorities in relationships, there are certain people in our lives with whom we do have a covenant understanding. These relationships are usually with the people closest and most important to us, and between us is an understood covenant of our promises and commitments to that relationship.

What is a covenant relationship? I think the best definition of a covenant relationship, one that encompasses the full range of relationships, is as follows:

A covenant relationship is one where no one else can adequately or properly fulfill your role in that relationship. Your contribution is unique and vital.

For example, no one can be your children's mother or father except you. No one can fully take my place in the lives of my parents. I can't say to my two brothers, "I'm tired of being a sister; find someone else to take my place." No one else can be my brothers' sister. That's my unique covenant relationship. No one can take my place as the mother of my daughter. If you are married, you have a covenant relationship with your mate, and you expressed that covenant in words at your wedding ceremony.

I realize that there are many situations where surrogates step in to take the place of a missing covenant relationship, such as foster parents, adoptive parents, etc. God often provides friends to help us when a covenant relationship is broken or missing. You've heard people say, "She's been like a mother to me," or, "He's like a son to me." In our broken world, it's wonderful that we can find substitutes, and those relationships can take on the characteristics of a covenant.

The Bible identifies some of our covenant relationships. The fifth commandment says, "Honor your father and your mother, so that you may live long in the land the Lord your God is giving you" (Ex 20:12). Obviously parent and child is a covenant relationship. The apostle Paul gave clear instructions on the responsibilities of husbands and wives in Ephesians 5:22-33. Theirs is a covenant relationship as well.

A covenant relationship is rarely defined by a legal contract and is not limited to blood relationships. It is usually a lifelong relationship, or at least one of very long duration. Whether or not the covenant has been expressed in words or in writing, it involves a clear understanding that this is not a take-it-or-leave-it relationship; it is one that requires commitment.

Besides the close members of my family, with whom I am obviously in covenant relationships, I have a few friends—my very closest friends—with whom I believe I share this kind of relationship. It's true, I'm not their only friend, but it's also true that in the case of these very few people, our friendships are so deep and so long-standing that no one could take their places in my life. I believe they would say the same of me. Because we share these covenant relationships, I feel a compelling loyalty and responsibility to them that is on the level of what I feel toward my family.

Which relationships in your life would fit the description of covenant relationship? You might find it helpful to actually write them down and even make an attempt to rank them according to the priority each has in your life. Some will undoubtedly share top billing, but in doing this ranking, do not go by whom you love the most but by where you have the greatest responsibility and commitment.

If you were asked to put in writing exactly what your covenant agreement is with these people on your list, would you be able to describe the parameters and responsibilities of that covenant? They begin with what the Word of God teaches us concerning our duties in these relationships, and it has a lot to say.

You may also be able to identify unique sets of commitments and duties for particular relationships. For example, a covenant relationship between a mother and a preschool child might look like this if written out:

I covenant with you, my son [daughter], to love you unconditionally, even when you behave badly, and to care for your welfare by feeding you, providing clothing for you, and assuring you a warm and safe place to live. I covenant to protect you from harm, to teach you how to grow up and be a godly adult, to guide you in your choices, to teach you God's Word, to correct you when you are in error, to punish you when you disobey, and to do everything I can to nourish you and help you achieve a life of integrity, character, and godliness.

Obviously, this covenant would change somewhat as this child ages, but many of the promises contained in it will last throughout that child's lifetime.

The words almost sound strange when you put down in writing what your commitment is to your covenant relationships, but I would encourage you to try it. You could go into much more detail or keep it very simple, but writing out that covenant will solidify in your own mind the priority of that relationship in your life.

With some of your covenant relationships, it might be very helpful to share your written covenant. Imagine how your child might feel if you put in writing your commitment to him or her. For a child who is old enough to understand what you're saying, this could form a bond and a security for him or her that will be very meaningful.

How about your mate? What would he or she think if you presented him or her with your covenant in writing? It might start to heal some wounds, open up some communication, or bring great comfort and joy to that person to whom you are married.

This exercise is probably one of the best things we could do to help us understand our responsibilities to our covenant relationships and thereby help us determine the priorities in our lives.

Maintaining a strong covenant relationship. Think of the precious covenant relationships in your life right now. These could include relationships with your mate, your child, a parent, a sibling, or some other extended family member who has been very close to you. Or one could be with a friend with whom you have developed a covenant relationship. What could you do today to let one of those covenant partners know how you feel about him or her? Here are some suggestions:

- Tell that person how glad you are God put him or her in your life. For example, out of the clear blue tell your child how glad you are God gave him or her to you. Especially when a child is small, he or she loves to hear about the day he or she was born and how excited you were to have that child in the family.
- Reaffirm your commitment to that person. It might be a shock to your mate, but wouldn't it be very nice for him or her to hear from you that the vows you took are just as important to you today as the first day you spoke them? Reaffirm your commitment to your marriage. That's a good thing for an anniversary celebration.
- Write a note expressing your appreciation for that covenant relationship. Whether the other person lives close by or not, putting your appreciation in writing really means a lot to people. Have you ever thanked your

parents in writing for all they've done for you? I guarantee you, they will treasure that letter.

- Do something special for a person with whom you share a covenant relationship—acting unexpectedly and for no reason at all—and just tell that person again, "It's just because I love you."

Covenant relationships should have the highest priority in our lives. Ask God to help you appreciate more the covenant partners in your life.

Contractual Relationships
The definition of a contractual relationship is the opposite of a covenant relationship. It is one in which the other person's place in your life can in fact be filled by someone else, even though that person may be important to you. We have many relationships in our lives that fall into this category. It's not that these relationships are unimportant; they simply are not exclusive.

Contracts are used in many ways in our society, usually in business settings. There are many written contracts, where the duties are spelled out, but there are also unwritten contracts, where duties and responsibilities are understood.

For example, when you accept a job with an employer, you may not have a written contract. You may not even have a written job description. But you have an understood contract that you will be at work on time, be honest, do the work you have agreed to do and the work assigned to you, show loyalty and respect to your employer, etc. Your employer also has understood responsibilities: to pay you as promised and on time, to give you the perks and benefits discussed, to treat you with respect and consideration, etc. Most if not all of the contractual relationships of our lives are unwritten.

The Bible gives us guidelines about what we owe to contractual relationships, and we've looked at some of those in detail.

We may owe a lot to our contractual relationships, but they should never have as high a priority in our lives as our covenant relationships do. If you get the priorities reversed, it can cause a great deal of harm and stress.

Your job is an important part of your life, but guess what: if you walk out tomorrow, somehow they'll survive without you. Your church is a vital part of your life, but when it's time for you to move on to another church or another job in the church, someone else will come along to fill the place you have left.

Certainly contractual relationships have importance, often great importance in our lives. Some are long-lasting, some are very dear, some are short, some are painful—they come in many different shapes and sizes. But they are not the highest priority in our lives because they are not covenant relationships.

It's also true that some covenant relationships have a higher priority in my life than others. After all, every relationship can't have the highest priority. It's also true that the relative priority placed on any particular covenant relationship can change with time and circumstance.

The point is, thinking of our relationships in terms of covenant and contract gives us a quick and helpful reminder of how our priorities should be placed.

In my early career with IBM, I was offered a promotion that required a great deal of travel. My daughter was still at home in school, and that travel would obviously take me away from her frequently. But I chose the promotion because I wanted the money and recognition that came with it.

As a result, I was away from my daughter far too much. I made sure she had good care, but nonetheless I rendered to Caesar what belonged to God. I put a contractual relationship ahead of a covenant one. It was a mistake.

We need to really crystallize in our own minds with whom we have covenant relationships and keep that in mind as we make decisions. Many problems arise in our relationships when we consistently put contractual ones ahead of those that involve a covenant. That will almost guarantee a deterioration of the covenant relationships, if not a complete breakdown.

Children whose parents have not made them their highest priority are often plagued with all kinds of emotional problems because they instinctively know that something is wrong in this most important relationship. They are born with a need for parental devotion and care, with a need for the security of that loving relationship. When they perceive that their welfare is not of the utmost importance to one or both of their parents, it is painful and destructive and can affect their entire lives.

However, we must avoid the paranoia of thinking that if we ever fail in a covenant relationship to do what we should do, we're responsible for ruining that person's life. We all fail in all of our relationships at some point and in some way. That's why we have to learn how to be reconciled and how to mend the broken relationships of our lives. Sin has brought destruction into the world, and that certainly includes relationships.

For example, single parents often think that any problem one of their children has is a direct result of divorce. But guess what: Kids have problems in the best of situations. We truly must not allow ourselves to think that any failure on our part is fatal. God is an expert at taking our failures and turning them around, and he is also marvelous at filling in the missing pieces where a covenant relationship has failed.

Personal Performance Review

Get out your paper and pencil again, and write down answers to the following questions.

- Can you think of a time when you have rendered to "Caesar" (your boss or company) what belonged to God? Describe it.
- Can you remember a time when you failed to render to "Caesar" what actually did belong to "Caesar"?

Now, write down a list of the relationships in your life that you consider to be covenant relationships.

Choose one of those covenant relationships and write out that covenant, detailing the commitment and obligations you have to that person. ("I covenant with _____ to _____.") If you need a little help in how to proceed, you can look at the example written out earlier in this chapter. When you have finished, ask yourself if it might be a good idea to share this with the other person in your covenant relationship.

What could you do in the next few days to reaffirm your covenant relationships and their priority in your life? (For example, telling the other person how glad you are God put him or her in your life, writing a note to express your feelings about this covenant relationship, or doing something unexpected as a special treat for this person.) Write down your planned action.

In what areas do you see a need to improve in "rendering to Caesar what belongs to Caesar"? List them. For help in thinking this out, refer back to the section of this chapter on "What We Owe to Our Employer."

Chapter 11

Biblical Principle #11
Working With Difficult People

Twelve men were selected to work together in a team effort to achieve a goal. The selection process was controlled by their manager, one who made no mistakes, so these were the right men for the job. The job was unlike any other in all of history. These twelve men (minus one) would eventually change the course of history as they set out to proclaim the gospel of Jesus Christ.

One might think that living and ministering with Jesus night and day for more than three years would mean the team spirit was always positive and the men had no problem getting along. We are told, however, of many times when they argued, complained, connived, or resented. They were often unequal to the task, with failures and misunderstandings and jealousies and greed. Yet they stayed together and eventually became what God knew they could be all along—a powerful witness to their Lord and Savior, Jesus Christ.

* * *

When we go to a job outside our homes, we typically spend eight hours a day with coworkers and managers with whom we might never voluntarily choose to spend one-third of our waking hours. But there we are—together! And even though we're Christians, we're not immune to the irritations, aggravations, and outright conflicts that can exist in these relationships.

As I traveled across the country for many years giving business seminars, I got the same response from all types of people when I asked what aspect of their jobs caused them the greatest stress. At the top of almost everyone's list was something like "the people I work with," "a coworker who's driving me crazy," or "demanding customers!"

Learning how to cope with these difficult relationships on the job is a key issue for Christians in the workplace because there's much more at stake than stress or productivity. These conflicts give us opportunities to demonstrate the power of Christ and show that his presence makes a real difference in our everyday lives. As we find solutions to these conflicts through application of Scripture, we provide testimony that cannot be discounted because most people never find any answers for these interpersonal difficulties.

It must be noted that there are many nonbelievers who are good hard workers, who do their jobs really well, and who are a pleasure to know and work with. We're not saying that any person who is not a Christian will be a difficult coworker. It's not true. Unfortunately it is also not true that a Christian will never be difficult.

But as Christians we have a motivation and a power that our nonbelieving coworkers don't have. Our motivation is to please Jesus and obey his principles, and our power is the Holy Spirit who indwells our bodies and gives us the ability to do what otherwise would be impossible. This gives us a great advantage over nonbelieving coworkers if we are willing to go God's way and allow his Spirit to control us.

That never should cause us to have an arrogant attitude, however—just the opposite. We should be humbled and made compassionate toward others as we recognize that by God's grace we have this advantage. We can therefore understand how big a struggle it is for anyone who doesn't have the power of God's Spirit to help them.

Following biblical principles will take us down very different roads than most of our nonbelieving coworkers would go. It will require the servant attitude that can come only through the power of God in our lives. We must be prepared to deal with difficult work relationships God's way, not our own defensive way.

Maybe you're thinking, *What? Are Christians supposed to be doormats? I don't buy that.* It doesn't sit well with me, either—with the "natural" me. But you know, more and more I'm coming to realize that if I choose to follow Christ and live by his principles, it will require a commitment that will appear radical and unreasonable at times: it will go against my natural reactions. I find that often we Christians rationalize away and water down God's principles, based on our own reasoning processes and the influence of this world's thinking on us.

You know what I mean. We think, *Sure, Jesus taught us to go the extra mile and love our enemies and all that, but he wasn't referring to this type of situation,* or, *I understand what Jesus is saying in Matthew 5, but it doesn't apply to this.* We begin to pick and choose our beliefs from Scripture to suit our own desires. We denounce others who deny the inspiration of Scripture and become their own judge of what is to be believed and what isn't, and yet we can be guilty of the same kind of selective interpretation, trying to make Scripture match our own preferred beliefs or lifestyles.

I find that often, even with all I know and all I teach, I can mentally excuse myself from obeying a biblical principle. I can teach the importance of biblical principles and then realize I'm failing to apply the teaching to my own life. I have to pull myself up short and say, "Hey, this means you!"

Please realize that God's principles in these relationships may be far more than you would ever do on your own, and even more than your employer requires of you. God's principles are higher, and we are held to a more righteous standard. The good news is that he empowers us to do what he requires us to do, by the Holy Spirit within us.

Therefore, if you're prepared to take the "road less traveled," you are in for some wonderful surprises and astonishing results. It's like Jesus told us: when you choose to lose your life, then you will find it. And by choosing to approach difficult relationships God's way, you are going to see new life in those relationships and a newness of life within you.

Dealing With Difficult Coworkers

You've probably noticed that the Bible doesn't have a chapter on "dealing with difficult coworkers." Nevertheless, there are five types of difficult coworkers we are likely to encounter, and the principles of Scripture can be directly applied to each of these relationships.

The Lazy Coworker

One of the more common types of difficulties we encounter with coworkers is the person who is lazy and doesn't pull his or her own weight in the workplace. This is the person who spends most of his or her day in personal phone conversations, fritters away time in trivial conversations, drinks more cups of coffee than you can count, or seems to be away from his or her desk most of the day. When you encounter this person on your job, you may find that relationship engenders some strong reactions—at least at times. For example, you may feel angry, experience a desire to get even, or find you have a tendency to gossip or drop sarcastic remarks about that person. You may even decide to slack off on your own work, doing no more than is required, and to quit being "Mr. Nice Guy." It's very easy to become bitter and resentful, and the wall between you and that coworker builds quickly under these circumstances.

As we consider how best to deal with lazy coworkers, we must first make certain that we keep our own hearts and attitudes in the right condition. God will hold us accountable for how we behave, regardless of what others do. We can't blame others for our inappropriate behavior. If you've let a relationship with a lazy coworker get to the resentful stage, then first begin to ask God to help you change your heart and attitude. That will be required before God begins to work on the other person!

There are times in such cases that we should "speak the

truth in love." Some indications that it is time to do so would
be that

- you realize that until this coworker truly changes, he or
  she will continue to inflict harm on you and others and
  will never become the good worker that he or she could
  be
- you realize that you are now enabling this coworker to
  continue doing wrong and are keeping him or her from
  learning to do what is right
- after much prayer, you have received a "green light" in
  your spirit from God, and you know it is time for you to
  take some action

Notice that the primary motivation here is the welfare of the
lazy coworker, other coworkers, or the company, as well as
yourself. Whom we are concerned about is one of our first
clues as to the purity of our motivation. You can have a pretty
good idea your motivation is off base if

- you are sick and tired of doing this lazy coworker's work
  and you realize you are going to explode if you don't say
  something soon
- this lazy coworker is taking advantage of you and even
  taking credit for the work that you're doing, and that
  isn't fair to you
- management has a totally wrong impression of this lazy
  coworker, and you believe it's time they knew the real
  story

If we are only concerned about ourselves in a situation like this, chances are we won't speak in love but rather in anger, frustration, defensiveness, or even self-righteousness. Then, even if the action is warranted and we speak the truth, it won't accomplish the good for which it was intended. How to instead speak the truth in love was discussed in chapter seven, where we dealt with constructive confrontation—you will be confronting the coworker with the effects of his or her lazy behavior.

Before acting, however, your first decision is whether or not you should speak to the coworker. Partly that decision will depend on your authority level, how much his or her poor work habits truly affect you, and other issues peculiar to each situation.

Here are some other approaches you could take in dealing with a lazy coworker. Note the potential pros and cons of each.

Allow the problem to surface on its own. Simply do your own work well, but don't do the other person's work. Eventually his or her poor work habits will come to the attention of those in power and hopefully will be addressed from an upper level position.

Pro: You don't have to take any action personally that could aggravate the lazy coworker and therefore cause him or her to be angry with you.

Con: Allowing the poor work to continue could cause harm to others, such as customers. Or it could cause serious problems with company policy, deadlines, etc. There's no guarantee that management will take the needed action.

Bring the matter to the attention of upper management. You might decide to do this if letting the work go undone would be harmful to some innocent people, like customers.

> Pro: The matter will be resolved by people who can do the right thing for the customer, who should have primary consideration.

> Con: Going directly to management could cause relationship problems with the lazy coworker and any others who learn that you "tattled"—and those things usually are found out.

Keep a record of the times when you have done the coworker's work. You will then have some proof of the problem when you decide the time is right to confront the situation.

> Pro: This would give you documentation of the problems caused by the lazy coworker, which is far more persuasive than words or feelings.

> Con: This approach could be viewed as very underhanded or subversive.

Hang in there a while longer. Go a few more extra miles without griping, complaining, or gossiping.

> Pro: There are times when God will lead you to simply hang on because he is doing something behind the scenes that you can't see. If there is a strong check

in your spirit, then you can trust that God is working it out in a better way than you ever could.

Con: The only downside to this alternative is the possibility of resentment setting in and spoiling your attitude.

As you consider the alternative approaches that could be used in dealing with a lazy coworker, I'm sure you realize that none of these are right or wrong. The situation will have to determine your course of action, depending on the people involved. That doesn't mean that you would not do what might be viewed as politically incorrect. God may want you to stick your neck out and take the risky road. But if you do that on your own instead of in God's power, you'll have a big mess on your hands.

Be sure to give these situations much, much prayer time, and constantly monitor your motives. What you must guard against is a build-up of bitterness, which can quickly happen when we're dealing with lazy coworkers. You can't blame bitterness on others. It's your responsibility and mine to keep that root of bitterness from growing within us.

The Condescending, Arrogant Coworker
A description of a condescending and arrogant coworker would include the following:
- talks down to people
- unteachable
- knows it all
- a "been there and done that" attitude

- name-dropper
- frequent body language and facial expressions that indicate aloofness, disgust, disapproval, and the like
- treats others as though they are stupid

When people have a continual attitude of arrogance and condescension, it is a telltale sign that underneath that intimidating outward appearance lies a great deal of insecurity and pain. It usually reveals a lack of confidence, a need for recognition, and a fear of rejection.

There are times when God may want you simply to bear with that person, not being intimidated by the behavior but trying to ignore it as much as possible. Then you may need to speak the truth in love to him or her—when God gives you the green light to do so.

Jesus taught us to love our enemies, and these arrogant coworkers give us ample opportunity to practice that principle. It's helpful to remember that we don't have to like them in order to love them. Loving them means acting toward them in considerate and loving ways, even though we may not feel it.

The Domineering Coworker

Have you ever worked with people who had delusions of greatness? They just seem to assume that they have a right to manage other people, even though they have not earned the position of manager.

I remember one woman who worked for me. She was a very thorough, conscientious worker, but she had an uncanny way of telling her coworkers that if they did things her way, the department would run much more smoothly. Now, in fact the quality of her work was superior to that of her peer, but she created a great deal of animosity and resentment in the department through her overbearing attitude. In fact, as her manager I even felt her attacks at time—and resented them! Domineering people can bring out the worst in us.

It can be particularly humbling to work or live with someone who is domineering and bossy. Everything in you wants to tell this person where to get off. You like to ask sarcastically, "Who made you king [or queen]?"

In Luke 14:11 Jesus exhorts us to humble ourselves: "For everyone who exalts himself will be humbled, and he who humbles himself will be exalted."

In 1 Peter 5:6 we see another promise given to us when we practice this principle: "Humble yourselves, therefore, under God's mighty hand, that he may lift you up in due time."

These passages give us two clear promises of what will happen when we are truly willing to humble ourselves: we will be lifted up, and we will be exalted. Don't miss Peter's phrase, "in due time." That's probably not as soon as you would like it to be, but it will be in the right time, after you have learned the valuable lesson of humbling yourself.

Meanwhile, there are some specific ways we can respond to such a coworker that will help us humble ourselves:

- Refrain from any verbal response.
- Be willing to do what they ask or demand, even though you are not required to do so.
- Respond in a quiet, controlled manner.
- Explain that you are not required to follow his or her instructions but you are going to do so anyway.

- Smile when he or she barks orders at you, and then ignore the orders.
- Refuse to join in any character assassination aimed at this coworker.

With a domineering coworker, it is humbling to keep your mouth shut and not bark back. It is even more humbling to take the direction and let the coworker get by with it! There may be times when that's the right thing for us to do with the domineering type. God is interested in developing Christlike characteristics in us, and sometimes he uses unfair and uncomfortable circumstances for that purpose.

Now, don't misunderstand me. I'm not necessarily saying that we should always take direction from these domineering people. But if a confrontation is called for, our motives have to be carefully examined to make certain we're confronting first of all for the other person's good, not just to vent our frustration.

Certainly there may be times when you will need to confront this type of coworker. But before you take any other action, ask God if there is some way you can learn to humble yourself through your relationship with this domineering coworker.

The Negative Coworker

I'm quite certain all of us have had to work with someone who was habitually negative! In fact, have you noticed that negative people are far more successful at making positive people negative than positive people are at making negative people positive? It only takes one negative, complaining person to get the whole workplace in negative mode. We go downhill much more easily than we go uphill, I guess.

There's a study that says, if we have a positive experience, we tell three people, but if we have a negative experience, we tell eleven. We all seem to be attracted to negativity. That's why the newspapers, television, and radio focus so much on the bad news rather than the good news. We buy bad news more than good news!

So we're going to be swimming upstream when we decide to be a positive person and not let the negative people around us drag us down, but it can be done, and believers in Jesus Christ should do it. After all, we have something to be positive about. In fact, this is one of our greatest opportunities to witness on the job—to simply maintain a positive attitude in the midst of a negative world.

How can you keep the negative people around you from pulling you down to their level? Here are some things I try to practice to help me stay positive:

- Recite out loud all I have to be thankful for. Remember every day all the good things in my life.
- Don't let little stuff get to me. If it isn't going to matter in twenty-four hours, I try to just let it go. It's little stuff—I find that much of what makes me negative won't matter this time tomorrow.
- Sing good Christian songs to myself. I try to fill up my mind throughout the day with good, positive things.
- Remember that I know the end of the story—Jesus wins. I have eternity in heaven with him because of his amazing grace, and if I can keep an eternal perspective in a

daily world, I won't find it so difficult to be a positive person.

- Say something positive every time that negative coworker says something negative. I know that attitudes are contagious, so perhaps they will catch my positive one instead of my catching their negative one.

- Don't spend any more time with a negative person than I have to, or than God directs me to! You don't want to eat lunch every day with the negative coworker. Just try to surround yourself with the positive people and positive inputs into your mind. That will help you stay positive.

When you are dealing with a very negative person, you will not find it easy to love that person, because his or her behavior will not naturally generate a compassionate response. In fact, it will likely generate hostility or disgust or anger. If you want to respond to a negative person in a biblical way, you will have to pray for the desire and the power to go the extra mile and treat that person with kindness.

In fact, some kind words spoken to that negative person might be the key to getting him or her past that negativity and into a more positive mode. Don't underestimate the power of your own words, and carefully select kind, positive words as a response. It not only may have a good effect on the difficult person, but it will also insulate your mind against their negativity so that you do not succumb and become negative yourself.

And then don't forget what Solomon taught us: "Do not speak to a fool, for he will scorn the wisdom of your words"

(Prv 23:9). There are people who are committed to being negative, and nothing is going to move them from that position. To try to change them is futile, and indeed that person will treat you with scorn. People who are totally negative and refuse to be otherwise are indeed very foolish. They heap untold misery on themselves and others. That type of "fool" will be offended and incensed by your positiveness, and any words of wisdom you give will be scorned.

The Vindictive, Hostile Coworker
Unfortunately there are people in this world who are intent on evil, and sometimes they show up where we work. These are the vindictive, malicious, and even vicious types who are openly trying to cause problems and do harm.

Jesus came to bring true light to the world, and when we become believers, he says that we are the light of the world (Mt 5:14). We become the bearers of his light into a very dark world. That is a great privilege, but it comes with its "downside," if you please.

This is the verdict: Light has come into the world, but men loved darkness instead of light because their deeds were evil. Everyone who does evil hates the light, and will not come into the light for fear that his deeds will be exposed.

JOHN 3:19-20

If the world hates you, keep in mind that it hated me first. If you belonged to the world, it would love you as its own. As it is, you do not belong to the world, but I have chosen you out of the world. That is why the world hates you.

JOHN 15:18-19

Jesus gives us clear warning of relationship problems that we will incur simply because we are believers in him and carry his light into our dark world. Why should it be different for us than it was for him?

We should not be shocked to discover that on occasion our Christian "light" will generate a hostile response from a coworker. Remember what Jesus told us in the above passage from John 3: the reason for this unpleasant reaction is the fear of exposure. That coworker is aware of your glaring light, exposing his or her evil ways, so that person strikes out against you to try to "kill the light." In response to your "light," that coworker could try to smear your reputation, make fun of you, tell lies about you, ignore you, embarrass you—you get the idea. Perhaps you've experienced that kind of treatment somewhere in your career. It is not pleasant.

But here is the good news, as given to us in 1 Peter 2:19-21:

For it is commendable if a man bears up under the pain of unjust suffering because he is conscious of God. But how is it to your credit if you receive a beating for doing wrong and endure it? But if you suffer for doing good and you endure it, this is commendable before God. To this you were called, because Christ suffered for you, leaving you an example, that you should follow in his steps.

A few years ago as I was memorizing this passage, the reality of this scripture began to dawn on me. Called to suffer unjustly? You've got to be kidding! I remember thinking, "Lord, I just don't think I'll ever be really willing to do that."

The only way we can learn to accept unjust suffering and treatment is to constantly remind ourselves that by doing so we have an opportunity to share in Jesus' suffering, which gives us the great privilege of learning to follow in his steps.

Think about it: when you are going through tough waters, you feel very close to someone who's been there before you, because that person really knows what you're feeling. When we have an opportunity to taste the kind of suffering Jesus drank fully for us, then we know him better. And that in turn brings his resurrection power into our lives in greater measure.

Jesus was being remarkably revolutionary when he said:

Blessed are you when people insult you, persecute you and falsely say all kinds of evil against you because of me. Rejoice and be glad, because great is your reward in heaven, for in the same way they persecuted the prophets who were before you.

MATTHEW 5:11-12

If you have sincerely suffered from relationships on your job simply because you take a stand as a believer, or live a Christian lifestyle, you are to consider it a compliment! You are not to

184 / *Getting Along With People @ Work*

get angry or vengeful or guilty; rather you are to rejoice and be glad. Whoa! That should come as a great relief to us. It takes the monkey off our back and the sting out of the suffering.

However, please don't use this as an excuse for poor behavior on your part! I can remember times when I wanted to believe that I was being picked on because I was a Christian, but in reality, my behavior was not very Christian. So, when our own poor behavior causes people to treat us badly, that's one thing. But when we are persecuted by others just because we are a light in a dark world, we should have a real sense of joy inside of us that we would be counted worthy to suffer for Jesus, and that our lives do indeed have that effect on others.

Also, keep in mind that quite often people who have the most adverse reaction to a Christian witness or a Christian lifestyle are the ones under conviction, the ones who may be the closest to the Kingdom. It bothers them enough that they show their reaction, so you may want to redouble your prayer for those people. Who knows what God may be doing in their hearts?

Conclusion

I am reminded of what Jesus said to his disciples when they were having difficulty getting along with each other. James and John (and their mother) had tried some deceptive methods to win the Lord's favor, and when the other ten learned of it, they were indignant. Jesus recognized their conflict, and he sat them down and once again explained, "If anyone wants to be first, he must be the very last, and the servant of all" (Mk 9:35b).

A servant heart is the sum total of what we've been saying

here. It goes against our natural instincts, but then we are to be dead to that old person and alive unto Christ. As difficult as that is at times, it's much easier than doing it our way, and the benefits we reap are eternal ones.

Personal Performance Review

Ask yourself the following questions:

- Who is the most difficult coworker you now must work with on your job?
- What characteristics make this person difficult to work with? (You may find the person you are thinking about fits one or more of the categories discussed in this chapter, or you may add others.)
- What is your most common emotional reaction to this person? (Resentment, anger, desire for revenge, loss of your own motivation to work well, or something else?)
- What are you willing to do in order to have a Christlike attitude toward this person? (Pray for this person or for a changed attitude, humble yourself and not respond, respond with kindness instead of sarcasm, stop gossiping about this person, confront in love for his or her benefit, or other)

Chapter 12

Biblical Principle #12
Working With a Difficult Manager

There was a brilliant, promising young man who worked for a very demanding, dictatorial boss. He was in a job he did not choose or want, working for a man with whom he did not agree, in circumstances that were not friendly to his faith in God. Yet, in the midst of this, he was such a good worker that his boss found none equal to him, and he rose to prominence in that place.

His name was Daniel, and you will never find a better role model for getting along with a difficult manager. Forced into servitude by King Nebuchadnezzar, though he refused to bow his knee to the foreign gods, his honesty and work effort were recognized and honored by the king. Without compromising one iota in his dedication to the true God of Israel, he did the king's business with integrity and excellence, and eventually he had great influence over that very difficult king.

Most of us have earthly managers to whom we report. I've had quite a few in the course of my career. I have fond memories of some of these managers, and one or two can still make chills run up my spine!

Management relationships hold a particular challenge for

us because management has power and can influence the course of our careers, our incomes, and our work content—in other words, management can affect many important areas of our lives. Also, we have limited access to and influence with management, and as a friend told me early in my career, it is our job to get along with them rather than their job to get along with us!

It only makes sense that we should do whatever we can to improve and enhance our relationships with those in authority over us, given their impact on our lives. It would not be wise to antagonize or alienate the person or people who have this kind of power over us. Yet often these can be the most difficult relationships we encounter on the job.

Again, we want to begin with a clear understanding of biblical principles concerning these relationships, and believe it or not, the Bible has a lot to say about how you relate to your boss.

The Important Matter of Attitude

The first biblical principle we need to consider regards our attitude toward those in authority. While we recognize that position does not make anyone better than anyone else, Romans 13:1-2 gives us clear teaching on authority:

Everyone must submit himself to the governing authorities, for there is no authority except that which God has established. The authorities that exist have been established by God. Consequently, he who rebels against the authority is rebelling against what God has instituted, and those who do so will bring judgment on themselves.

God has established authority as part of the order of the universe. If it were not for the principle of authority, we would have nothing but chaos. The same is true in the business world. Authority is essential, and managers are part of God's plan. As Christians we are directed to submit ourselves to the people who have risen to positions of authority.

But we see so much evidence that many people in authority are neither godly nor competent. Can their authority be God-given? Yes, even though they may not use their position well or appropriately, their authority is nonetheless from God, and as Christians we are to respect it. To rebel against that is to rebel against God's order, and as Paul said, it will bring judgment on us.

Obviously there have been and are people in such positions who should never be there, but that was true when Paul wrote his Letter to the Romans. The principle still holds: we may not respect the people themselves, but we must respect their position and submit to them as long as they are in authority over us.

This is contrary to the times. In one of my business training classes, a woman said to me privately, "Mary, I'm older, and I treat my boss with lots of respect, do things for him that the other assistants don't do. The other women are angry with me for treating my boss like I do, and they keep telling me that it makes them look bad. What do you think?"

She was taught to respect authority almost to the point of fear. But during the '60s and '70s we saw a backlash against all authority, and that generation was taught to reject and challenge all authority. Romans 13, which tells Christians to submit to authority, seems very much outdated and out of place today.

But as Christians in the marketplace, it is where we start. First Peter 2:18 even says that we must submit not only to those masters who are good and considerate but also to those who are harsh, difficult, or unpleasant. The principle of submitting and respecting their authority still applies. If we're not willing to apply that biblical principle, we will invite trouble into our lives.

Remember, you apply this principle by faith, not by feelings. You pray it into your life on a daily basis. You ask God to change your attitude and change your thinking so that you can accept that authority. Easy? No. Effective? Yes. It works, and when you apply this principle, you're in a position for God to bless you. Furthermore, he may even change the situation. But whether or not it changes, you will find freedom through obedience.

Pray for Your Management
Another extremely important principle in improving our relationships with our management is found in 1 Timothy 2:1-2:

> I urge, then, first of all, that requests, prayers, intercession and thanksgiving be made for everyone—for kings and all those in authority, that we may live peaceful and quiet lives in all godliness and holiness.

We are to pray for those in authority, and we are to pray for peaceful relationships with them. Notice that your relationship with those in authority is relevant to your own spiritual condition. Praying for those in authority is essential to a peaceful and quiet life.

Have you been praying for your boss or bosses regularly? This is where it starts, and until you truly begin to pray for those in authority over you, you won't see much change in your attitude or in their behavior.

What is the best way to pray for those in authority? First, pray for their spiritual condition. Pray that they will come into saving faith with Jesus Christ, if they have not already. Pray that they will make righteous decisions, that they will manage for the good of the company, its employees, and its customers. Pray for their families, as much as you know about them.

Also pray for your attitude toward them. Pray that you will respect their authority (whether you respect the person or not) and that you will submit to their authority appropriately. Pray that God will help you to see this person or these people the way he sees them. Ask him to help you see beyond the irritations, inconveniences, or frustrations they cause you and to see the eternal purpose of that relationship in your life.

This kind of praying is guaranteed to improve your relationship with management. It will also give you a compassionate understanding you've never had before, reduce stress you may experience in that relationship, make you a better employee doing better work, and bring peace and quiet into your heart and life, regardless of what's going on around you on the job.

Protect Your Boss

Smart employees understand that their unwritten job description includes making their boss look good. The world uses that principle as a manipulative tool, but we have other reasons for it. First Corinthians 13:6-7 describes the kind of love we are to develop in our lives, a love that is like God's love.

That kind of love "does not delight in evil but rejoices with the truth. It always protects, always trusts, always hopes, always perseveres."

As Christians we are ever to be seeking to have God's love fill us and overflow through us to everyone in our lives, including our bosses. Therefore we should try to make them look good, not for manipulation purposes but because God's love motivates us to protect others from bad exposure, to delight in the good things they do, not the bad things, and to try to cover up their mistakes whenever we can. This certainly doesn't mean that we should be a part of any illegality or improper cover-up, but it does mean that we don't take part in the gossip or character assassination that is so commonly voiced about management.

Solomon gives us some good advice about how we talk about those in authority:

Do not revile the king even in your thoughts, or curse the rich in your bedroom, because a bird of the air may carry your words, and a bird on the wing may report what you say.

ECCLESIASTES 10:20

If you talk about your boss behind his or her back, you can be assured it will get back to that person sooner or later. Birds on the wing may report what you say! It is very unwise to participate in this kind of back-stabbing talk, and it is unkind and unloving.

The Unreasonable or Incompetent Boss

Someone once told me that you can learn as much from an incompetent or bad manager as you can from a good one, and I think that's probably true. But the learning is more difficult and painful! I get many letters telling me sad stories of trying to work for a boss who is lazy, disorganized, inexperienced, or unqualified for his or her job. Others work for a boss who uses methods that are unethical, ineffective, or contrary to company policy. They are usually sadly lacking in "people skills," and they are not willing to accept suggestions or help from anyone else.

What is our Christian responsibility when we work for this type of person? Solomon again has some good advice: "Through patience a ruler can be persuaded, and a gentle tongue can break a bone" (Prv 25:15). Even though your anger toward your "ruler" may be justified, you need to lengthen it. Stretch it out; don't have a short fuse. And most importantly, keep a soft tongue. Through patience and a gentle tongue a ruler can be persuaded. If you want to change your boss's behavior toward you, pray this biblical principle into your life, and watch what happens.

Consider again what Peter tells us:

> Slaves, submit yourselves to your masters with all respect, not only to those who are good and considerate, but also to those who are harsh. For it is commendable if a man bears up under the pain of unjust suffering because he is conscious of God. But how is it to your credit if you receive a beating for doing wrong and endure it? But if you suffer for doing good and you endure it, this is

commendable before God. To this you were called, because Christ suffered for you, leaving you an example, that you should follow in his steps.

1 PETER 2:18-21

We discussed this passage in respect to dealing with a difficult coworker who purposely tries to harm us. The same applies when that coworker is our boss. Notice again the special reward that is ours when we deal with an unreasonable manager in this patient manner. We find favor with God and we follow in the steps of Jesus. Please consider the impact of those two special rewards.

Finding Favor With God

This means God is pleased with you, that you bring joy to his heart, that you bring honor and glory to God when you bear up under an unreasonable manager with patience and grace and kindness. I can absolutely guarantee you that finding favor with God far outweighs any pain or frustration created by your manager's behavior. You will be able to accept that manager, even to pity him or her, when you realize that a proper response on your part finds favor with God.

In my first book, *The Christian Working Woman*, written many years ago, I have a chapter entitled "The Impossible Boss." I tell there of my experience with a difficult boss, whose management style was intimidating and humiliating to me. How much God taught me through that relationship! Now I can honestly say that it was one of the best things God did in order to bring me to maturity and prepare me for the ministry ahead.

One of the key things I learned in dealing with this boss was to see past his behavior and understand his personal dilemma. I remember sitting in meetings afterward, observing the behavior that previously had caused me such frustration and pain and now feeling so sorry for him because he didn't have a personal relationship with Jesus and the peace and joy that comes through him alone.

Once I began to practice this principle of seeing him the way God sees him, my stress was immediately and dramatically reduced, my patience was lengthened, and I found favor with God. You know you find favor with God when there is that peace inside of you that cannot be explained. You know you find favor with God when you are no longer personally irritated by unfair treatment and you see yourself responding with grace and kindness.

Knowing that you find favor with God is sweeter than words can describe. Hopefully you've experienced this somewhere along the way and you know what I'm talking about. It is worth more than anything else, and you can actually get to the place where you thank God for the difficulty that has brought you to a place where you find favor with him.

Following in the Steps of Jesus

Dealing with an unfair, unreasonable, or incompetent manager in a patient and kind way allows you to have a unique relationship with Jesus. That's because you are experiencing the kind of suffering he experienced—unjust suffering.

I would never choose suffering; neither would you. But when unjust suffering comes your way and you are able to see it as an instrument in the hand of God, you will discover the incredible privilege of sharing in the same kind of suffering Jesus endured.

I wish I could find adequate language to describe this to you, because it is difficult to understand or believe until you have experienced it. Any circumstance that brings you to the place where you are willing to endure unjust suffering because that is what God wants you to do becomes a blessing in your life. And that includes your difficult, impossible, unreasonable, unfair, incompetent boss!

Of course that doesn't mean your boss's behavior is right. It doesn't justify or whitewash inappropriate management styles. It does allow you to do as Joseph did—to turn what was meant for evil into an instrument of good. As Joseph put it, "You intended to harm me, but God intended it for good to accomplish what is now being done, the saving of many lives" (Gn 50:20).

You see, the enemy of your soul, Satan, would love to destroy your testimony and steal your joy through this difficult relationship. But when you turn the table on Satan, that thief and liar, and instead allow God to turn it into something good, you defeat the forces of hell. Let me tell you, that's a really good feeling!

God may lead you to take some action to expose or try to change unfair management practices. He may instruct you to confront your manager for the good of the company and other workers. But before you go there, make sure you give God permission to change your heart and to bring you to this place of being willing to suffer unjustly for his sake. It's an experience like no other, and it will give you a depth of maturity in your walk with God that nothing else can do. You really don't want to miss it!

Personal Performance Review

If you work for a difficult manager, what is your main issue with him or her? (For example, incompetence, poor communication, or unreasonable expectations.)

What can you do—or what are you willing to do—to have a Christlike attitude toward this manager? (For example, pray for him or her, pray that your attitude will become one of submission to authority, or do what you can to protect him or her.)

Chapter 13

Biblical Principle #13

The Joy of Improved Relationships

If you are a results-oriented person, as I am, you're always looking for a bottom-line story. OK, I ask, so I work hard and try to really improve my work relationships. So I pray for God's grace to put others first and love unconditionally and go the extra mile and confront constructively. So what difference does it make?

The most important difference is the joy of obedience. I'm sure you've already discovered in your own walk with the Lord that when you are living in obedience, your joy is full. If you are a parent, you know how pleasant and enjoyable life is at home when the children are doing as asked, following instructions. You are able to enjoy the good things about family life in far greater measure. The challenge is to help your children understand and believe that obedience is better for them too!

The same is true in our relationship with our Father God. Obedience is much better for us! If that were the only benefit, it would be enough. But there's more. God gives us his principles for good reason—they work and ours don't. So when you live in obedience to his principles regarding relationships, you will discover that life is much easier and more comfortable for you because those sandpaper relationships are greatly improved.

In case you are still not convinced, however, or you just need a little more encouragement, I wanted to end the book with a few stories of people I know who have seen God work miracles and change relationships on their jobs as they obeyed his principles.

Steve's Story

My friend Steve is now a pastor on staff at our church. Before going to seminary, though, Steve spent ten years in the workplace—a highly recommended experience for anyone going into ministry—as a manager for a well-known trucking company, supervising about twenty union drivers.

As he went into the job, he began to realize that the underlying attitude, both for supervisors and drivers, was an "us versus them" attitude. It was assumed that you could not have truly congenial relationships between supervisors and drivers. Any niceties were superficial, with much underlying mistrust. It was a strife-ridden atmosphere. Many drivers were not motivated to do more than they had to do, and the managers were constantly on their backs to get those packages delivered on time.

At first Steve followed suit and behaved as expected of managers, dealing with the drivers in a demanding and rough manner. But he soon realized this was not working, and he began to ask himself what he could do to motivate the unmotivated. Since he was a committed Christian, Steve knew he was to show Christian love and concern for the men and women that he supervised because God loved and valued them. So he decided to challenge the prevailing attitude by instead building relationships with the drivers whom he supervised.

He began by getting to know the men and women individually. He asked about their families. If there was a problem, he showed concern and did what he could. He took time occasionally to eat with them, and he made it a point to be available to them. In other words, he began to build bridges of friendship.

Because Steve would refuse to lie or participate in any kind of deception, he began to get a reputation among his fellow supervisors. He often irritated them because he wouldn't go along with their plans to lie or do something unethical, but they respected him for his stand. Before long they began to refer to Steve as "God-boy," but it was a term of endearment as they recognized the difference in Steve.

He wasn't preaching the gospel during lunch or handing out tracts every morning. He was trying to live out a loving attitude toward people, as Christ would have done.

There were certainly many times when he had to reprimand his employees. Some just wanted to get by with as little work as possible, and Steve knew it was his responsibility to demand an appropriate level of productivity from them. He says it was a constant struggle to find that right balance between demanding what was expected and at the same time having a caring attitude toward the drivers as individuals. That took a lot of prayer and wisdom from the Lord, and when Steve did confront, he was careful to do so in nonembarrassing ways, with carefully chosen words.

Steve is quick to remind me that he didn't do everything right and that his motives were not always pure. He remembers one occasion when he lost his temper and barked at an employee in a harsh and angry manner. This kind of thing was routine in that company, but Steve knew he had acted inappropriately. He went to the driver and apologized for his lack of control. Tears welled up in this man's eyes, and he said to Steve, "You didn't have to do that." (By the way, Steve went back to see his friends a few months after leaving, and this man informed him then that he has become a believer in Jesus Christ.)

Another man in his group, whose performance was continually below par, was called into a meeting with Steve and two other managers. As the three managers began to recite his shortcomings, the driver replied defensively that he was a Christian and he did good work because he was a Christian.

Knowing this was not the truth, Steve quietly asked the other managers if they would give him a few minutes alone with him. Once they were alone, Steve confronted the driver, not as manager to employee but as a brother in Christ. He spoke the truth in a loving way to him, explaining how management viewed him. He said that the managers, who were not Christians, perceived him as a loafer with a bad attitude. Steve explained that he needed either to change his work habits and make them what they should be or quit being so vocal about his faith in Christ, because he was not a credit to the name of Jesus Christ.

This employee took Steve's admonition to heart. He immediately went to the other managers and apologized for his failures, promising to improve. They were astonished and asked

Steve what in the world he had said to this guy to get him to apologize. Steve responded, "Well, we speak the same language."

Steve's success in dealing with this man and the other drivers was a result of the relationships he had established and the trust he had built over time. When he left to go to seminary, the union men threw him a party, gave him a Bible, and genuinely hated to see him leave. Steve's manager told him that never before had the union men had a party for a manager. It was unheard of. Returning a few months after he left for a visit, he was amazed that these big husky guys gave him hugs and asked when he was coming back!

Steve says there were many times when, out of frustration, he lost his patience or acted inappropriately, but he refused to accept the status quo. Instead he related to his workers in a Christlike way, putting them first, showing unconditional love, listening to their needs, and confronting constructively. These are God's principles, and they worked in Steve's situation in a remarkable way. Through applying them, he left behind him a strong testimony to the difference that Jesus makes in a life.

Cynthia's Story

My friend Cynthia works in a large bank in Chicago. She is a diligent worker and a disciple of Jesus Christ who truly sees her job as her mission field.

At one point she worked with a woman—we'll call her Janet—whom she considered to be a good friend. They had a nice enough working relationship and often shared meals and other moments of friendly conversation.

Cynthia was the only African-American in the department, but she had never considered that to be an issue and thought that her coworkers felt the same way. In a casual conversation, however, Janet remarked to Cynthia, "We can never really be friends because you're black." It shocked Cynthia to realize that this woman still would have such a bigoted attitude, even after knowing her so long.

Obviously it was painful for Cynthia, and she was tempted to just let the relationship go. After all, who needs it! (I'm sure I would have reacted that way.) She also began to view the other white members of her department with suspicion, imagining that they were all prejudiced toward people of color.

But God gave Cynthia different instructions, including the idea of starting Project Love. This involved inviting each of her coworkers to lunch, one per week, her treat. The purpose was to give Cynthia a chance to get to know her white coworkers and for them to get to know her.

She also realized that she was allowing Janet's attitude to create a wrong attitude in her, so Project Love was as much to keep her own attitude right as it was to help others have the right attitude toward her. In time, Cynthia saw how God used Project Love to build closer relationships in the department and to help her see her coworkers in nonjudgmental ways.

Then Cynthia decided she needed to confront Janet about her remark. She did so after her anger and resentment were past, but she told her how the comment had affected her and wondered why Janet would feel that way. That opened up a long conversation about Janet's prejudiced attitude toward African Americans, and Cynthia realized Janet's parents and extended family had handed this down to her.

Eventually Janet apologized to Cynthia and confessed that her attitude was wrong. She confirmed that indeed Cynthia was a good friend and that she valued her friendship greatly.

Even though they no longer work together, the two women still remain in contact. In fact, Janet never fails to send Cynthia a birthday card. On one occasion, Cynthia was thanking her for the card and Janet said, "Oh, Cynthia, you're just like family. Of course I don't forget your birthday!"

Janet had come a long way, thanks to Project Love and Cynthia's willingness to let go of the hurt and address the issue in an open and loving way. What could have been nothing but a painful memory is instead a victorious story of how God can change relationships when you're willing to go the extra mile, and give up your "rights" to be treated appropriately.

LaVerne's Story

LaVerne worked in a laboratory for many years. She was well experienced, hardworking, and productive, and she had a wonderful attitude. In short, she was the kind of worker everybody would want.

Then she encountered a coworker—we'll call her Linda—who would fit the description in chapter eleven of an abusive person, out to destroy whoever was in her way. Linda was ambitious and intent on getting to the top fast, and LaVerne was in her way.

Linda began a campaign of lies and deceptions about LaVerne as she cultivated the politically correct relationships with upper management. In spite of LaVerne's long, sterling track record, Linda was able to poison the minds of those in charge against LaVerne, and LaVerne endured much unfair treatment.

LaVerne desperately wanted to set the record straight, but as she prayed about this difficult relationship, the word from the Lord was "Wait." It turned out to be a two-year wait, and during that time she had to face Linda daily, knowing how she was deliberately trying to ruin LaVerne's reputation. LaVerne prayed a great deal during this time, and God gave her the ability to wait and not lash back at Linda.

After two years the truth began to surface. An unexpected illness put Linda in the hospital and kept her out of work for several months. Then management finally saw through Linda's lies and deception, and it became apparent that LaVerne had been doing the work that Linda took credit for.

God honored LaVerne for her patience, and she received an outstanding award for her service to the organization and, most meaningful to LaVerne, a glowing letter of praise from her manager. By allowing God to fight her battle for her instead of seeking her own revenge, LaVerne saw the salvation of the Lord. Linda, on the other hand, never realized her ambitions and subsequently was forced to retire.

Dorothy's Story

Dorothy worked at a mission agency and was in charge of administering the employment qualification tests to applicants. After the tests were completed, she would score them and then share the scores with the human resources director, along with any thoughts or impressions she had of the candidates. The director would then hold a formal interview with each candidate who had achieved passing scores.

Dorothy assumed that her comments—merely additional input to be used in evaluating applicants—were kept confidential.

One day Dorothy administered the tests to a young lady whose comments, way of taking the test, and test scores made Dorothy feel she might not be right for the job. She shared her concerns with the human resources director, though she assured him that she would do her best to train and help this person if they did decide to hire her.

They did hire her (we'll call her Marilyn), and Dorothy was assigned to begin training her. During the first few weeks Dorothy noticed that they were not getting along very well. Marilyn did not respond to Dorothy's training efforts, and she was rude and very cold in her dealings with Dorothy.

Dorothy had never had anyone respond to her in this way before, and she prayed about this for quite some time, asking why the Lord would send someone like Marilyn to their department when she just didn't fit in.

Things began to go from bad to worse. Marilyn even had a fellow employee taking sides with her. Dorothy just couldn't imagine what she had done to deserve being treated this way.

Finally Dorothy confronted Marilyn and asked, "Have I done something to you? I can't figure out why you dislike me." Marilyn's response was shocking. "When I was being interviewed, Don told me the things you said about me. He said that you didn't want me working in the department with you. Then when I started in the department, it seems like you are the office manager's pet and you can do no wrong."

Dorothy was upset and concerned that her comments, given in strictest confidence, had been passed on to Marilyn. Dorothy asked Marilyn if they could talk about it, but she did not want to do that.

Dorothy went home in tears and talked with her husband, who prayed with her. She asked the Lord to help her act in ways that would help Marilyn see that Dorothy did not dislike her.

Nevertheless things continued to get worse. Finally a confrontation was arranged, with the office manager, the human resources director, Marilyn, and Dorothy all present. Dorothy thought this would make the director realize the trouble he had caused by passing her remarks on to Marilyn. She thought, "The Lord will work things out the way I would like them to be (which was having Marilyn quit because I was there first and I wasn't going to quit!)"

At the meeting Dorothy told the human resources director that by passing on her confidential remarks he had sabotaged her working relationship with Marilyn even before it began. He didn't see it that way, however, and the meeting ended with the director telling Marilyn that she needed to change her attitude and telling Dorothy to accept Marilyn. Both women left the office feeling as though nothing had been accomplished.

One day shortly afterward, after others had left for lunch, Marilyn asked to talk with Dorothy. She said that Dorothy was different from what she thought she was. She noticed that Dorothy always tried to be nice to her, even when she was being difficult, and she was interested in hearing why. They talked through that lunch hour and many more after that. Eventually Dorothy was able to tell her how much God loved her and how he wanted her to know him.

After that Marilyn and Dorothy became rather good friends. Marilyn left the job after two years and began working closer to her home, but she would still call Dorothy if she had questions or needed help with things. Later she came back and worked as a part-time employee for a few months, and the two had a wonderful time.

Dorothy says, "I don't know if she has accepted the Lord as her personal Savior or not, but she is in my prayers continually. As I look back on the experience now, I thank the Lord for the lessons he taught me. Believers and nonbelievers are viewing our lives every day. We must be conscious of what we are doing. Our actions might be the thing that is keeping someone from knowing God's love fully."

Conclusion

I hope you have found this book to be practical and enlightening as you think about your work relationships. I would encourage you to choose one or two things you want to work on right now.

If we try to do too much at a time, we fail and become discouraged. So think of just one or two areas where you know you need to improve in relating to the people on your job, and start praying about those specific areas. Then by God's grace put his principles into action in your life.

I promise that the results will encourage you greatly. As your skills improve in dealing with people, your stress levels will go down, your productivity will go up, your enjoyment of your job, your family, your children, and your life will be enhanced, and most importantly, your testimony for Jesus Christ will be strengthened.

The great news is that when we are born from above, we have the power of the Holy Spirit to enable us to put God's principles into practice. As the apostle Paul reminded us in his First Letter to the Thessalonians, "The one who calls you is faithful and he will do it" (5:24).

Isn't that incredible? God calls us to a life of holiness, to a servant attitude, to putting others first, and to being compassionate, none of which come naturally to us. So Paul says, the one who calls you to this life—the Lord Jesus himself—will be faithful to do what he has called you to do.

It's one of the amazing paradoxes of the Christian life—we can't, but he can. Remember this:

He never said that I could, and I never can.
He promises that he can, and he always does.

I pray that you will see some great improvement in your relationships because of the power of God in you. I close with these words from the apostle Paul:

We ought always to thank God for you, brothers, and rightly so, because your faith is growing more and more, and the love every one of you has for each other is increasing.

2 THESSALONIANS 1:3

May that be true of all of us.